FREUD'S COUCH
SCOTT'S BUTTOCKS
BRONTË'S GRAVE

Also in the Culture Trails series

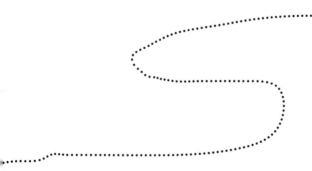

FREUD'S COUCH
SCOTT'S BUTTOCKS
BRONTË'S GRAVE

Simon Goldhill

UNIVERSITY OF CHICAGO PRESS

Chicago and London

SIMON GOLDHILL is professor of Greek literature and culture and fellow and director of studies in classics at King's College, Cambridge, as well as director of the Cambridge Victorian studies group. He is the author of many books, including *Love, Sex, and Tragedy: How the Ancient World Shapes Our Lives.*

The University of Chicago Press, Chicago 60637
The University of Chicago Press, Ltd., London
© 2011 by The University of Chicago
All rights reserved. Published 2011.
Printed in the United States of America

20 19 18 17 16 15 14 13 12 11   1 2 3 4 5

ISBN-13: 978-0-226-30131-0 (cloth)
ISBN-10: 0-226-30131-1 (cloth)

Library of Congress Cataloging-in-Publication Data

Goldhill, Simon.
    Freud's couch, Scott's buttocks, Brontë's grave / Simon Goldhill.
        p.   cm. — (Culture trails)
    ISBN-13: 978-0-226-30131-0 (cloth : alk. paper)
    ISBN-10: 0-226-30131-1 (cloth : alk. paper)
        1. Literary landmarks—Great Britain.   2. Scott, Walter, Sir, 1771–1832—
Homes and haunts—Scotland.   3. Wordsworth, William, 1770–1850—Homes
and haunts—England.   4. Brontë, Charlotte, 1816–1855—Homes and haunts—
England—Haworth.   5. Shakespeare, William, 1564–1616—Homes and haunts—
England—Stratford-upon-Avon.   6. Freud, Sigmund, 1856–1939—Homes and
haunts—England—London.   7. Great Britain—Description and travel.   I. Title.
II. Series: Culture trails.
PR110.G7G65 2011
820.9—dc23

                                                               2011026959

⊗ This paper meets the requirements of ANSI/NISO
Z39.48-1992 (Permanence of Paper).

CONTENTS

ACKNOWLEDGEMENTS

Great thanks to my traveling companions, who also read the draft chapters, David and Helen Stone and Daniel Eilon.

Deep thanks also to my colleagues in the Cambridge Victorian Studies Group, Clare Pettitt and Peter Mandler, who read and made helpful comments on the manuscript, as did Miriam Leonard, as ever. I discussed it all with Helen Morales, who is on a pilgrimage of her own. The readers for the University of Chicago Press were exceptional for the understanding they evinced in their reports and the trouble they took in reading with such care.

Most profound thanks to my wife, for traveling, reading, and putting up with the whole project. She found several new ways to articulate "Reader, I married him" during the composition of this book.

I

THE GOLDEN TICKET

I HAVE NEVER STOPPED being slightly anxious about the premise of this book. "Make a pilgrimage," proposed my editor over a grilled tuna salad. "Go anywhere and write about it." It sounds at first like a golden ticket. A set of destinations rose like a sunrise in my mind. The romance of the dusty open road, or at very least a Kerouac fantasy, is part of the adolescent mind of everyone of my generation. The mysterious traveler who blows into town, the life-changing encounter with a stranger, never forgotten, never recovered, the slow climb that reveals the breathtaking view—we all share these cultural myths, as we trudge to work or sit halfheartedly at the desk.

The trouble is that any really serious pilgrim travels alone. You are meant to make a journey where the very traveling leads you to explore yourself, your relation to God, or your life or your past. The endpoint is somehow only a small part of the process of inward transformation. This sort of pilgrimage started with the early Christians. A woman called Egeria left France and went to the Holy Land in the fourth century. It is boggling to imagine how hard it must have been, even with the securities of the Roman Empire and its straight roads and military checkpoints, for a woman to travel alone, as a Christian when Christianity was still a precarious institution, across such a distance and in such conditions. But not only did she make it there and back, she also wrote an account for her fellow sisters of the Church, telling of her tearful, overwhelmed response to the sites of the Passion, and of the services and worship she saw. It is one of the very first bits of prose we have written by a woman, and it now survives just in fragments, a tattered glimpse of her journey across deserts and darkness toward her enlightenment. I have a soft spot too for Prudentius, the fourth-century Christian Latin poet from Spain, who describes stopping in a church on his solitary trip to Rome, where he lay on the ground in front of the picture of a saint, weeping and wailing all afternoon at the image of martyrdom. That's how pilgrims do it—on bloodied knees, crawling toward an epiphany of self-awareness.

But I don't like being on my own. Although I am an academic who loves to spend all day in the library, and I get very jumpy if I don't get those long reading hours, nonetheless I don't like to eat alone, drink alone, sleep alone, walk alone, or even be silent for long. (I am not necessarily the person you want to sit next to in the library.) But if you go on a pilgrimage with a bunch of mates, I thought to myself, it is bound to turn into a comedy. You end up with Three Men in a Boat (and Montmorency the dog). Or Chaucer's pilgrims—a bawdy, sexy, drunken crew who started from a pub for a good time out together, telling stories all the way. Even Robert Louis Stevenson, an intense and self-absorbed young man, found that his journey of self-discovery veered into comedy the moment he decided to travel with a donkey (called Modestine, and the real star of his *Travels with a Donkey*). When you are no longer alone, instead of the Kerouac moment on the open road, it's Cliff Richard singing, "We're all going on a summer holiday," or *Little Miss Sunshine*. I had no desire to go there. Travel with a group might just be able to escape comedy, I supposed, but only at the expense of something worse: I knew the shuffling lines at Lourdes, the coach parties in Jerusalem, intently following the upheld umbrella toward the photo op of spirituality. I had no desire to go there either.

My first attempt to find some middle ground between lonely, despairing self-analysis and group pranks involved me sidling up to my wife, the lawyer. She is used to cutting through the desperate prose of her opponent's hopeful arguments. "You want me to be the straight woman to your pilgrim wit," she sniffed. "Or you want me to be the dumb American, while you expound on the history of places older than my country. Unattractive invitation. I'm not taking time off work for that." (Lawyers do not think of time like you or I do. There is no place for pleasure, let alone a journey of self-discovery. Time is divided simply into billable hours and nonbillable hours.) As I further reflected—aloud, stupidly enough—that a pilgrimage with one's wife would mean a journey of discovery into the complexities of marriage, a portrait of one's soul mate, so the prospect of a road trip for two—*It Happened One Night? Thelma and Louise?*—receded further and further. So I decided that what I needed to do was to make up a party of four Jews. To be four Jews on a train would have the structure of a joke—that would deal with the comedy—but you could guarantee that one of us at least would always be depressed and overintellectualize the occasion.

While I was ruminating on how a one might organize a modern, gregarious, uncomic pilgrimage, I was also struggling with the more pressing concern of where I wanted this pilgrimage to go. Each of my friends had a view, and expressed it firmly with growing excitement, as their imagination toyed with the golden ticket. I had quickly ruled out the natural world: Ayers Rock may be reached by a dusty road, but I couldn't see any mileage in a trip to such a hokey site of spiritual transformation. I had already written two books about Jerusalem, and the trip to get there is nothing, these days, in comparison to the difficulty of living there (unless you come from the occupied territories, and that would be a different project altogether, especially for four Jews). I could contemplate visiting the Ganges or Mount Fuji or any one of a host of pilgrimage sites my friends came up with, but the trip would be marred for me by the relentlessly touristy nature of such a project—I could only ever experience it as a rank outsider, baffled by the holiness of cows or nodding politely at awe before cherry blossoms. I was afraid that all I could do would be to smile at my own inability to escape from the stereotypes I already had—or end up like a Westerner in a sari, sadly mimicking a longed-for mystique. I wanted a trip that wouldn't leave me gaping or aping.

My editor came to my rescue. "Do something Victorian," she said. I had been nattering right through the tuna salad about the thrill of my new project on nineteenth-century ideas of the past, and my research group in Cambridge, and how great it was to be paid to read Victorian novels. Her insight was brilliant. Pilgrimage was all over the place in Victorian Britain, but not in the way we might immediately expect. The notion of a Victorian pilgrimage set me whirring with excited ideas and plans. The disappointment on the faces of my friends—no islands off the coast of Morocco? no elephants?—made me realize that I needed first to explain how pilgrimage became a Victorian fad, and why this pilgrimage would lead us into some amazing territory.

Let me start with some very general background, and, with pilgrimage, we are bound to start with religion. The nineteenth century experienced the fiercest arguments and conflicts over religion since the Reformation. Bred as we are to *Masterpiece Theatre* or BBC costume dramas, which always seem to find serious religion embarrassing or perturbing, this part of nineteenth-century culture has been rather swept under the carpet these days. But Britain, for most of the century at least, was staunchly Protestant, and the connection of church and state helped make the church an absolutely integral part of the social and intellectual life of the country, as well as providing its religious framework. Until decades into the century, only professed Anglicans could enter university or Parliament, and the battle to allow others—Nonconformists, Catholics, Jews—into these institutions of power was a nasty and protracted one (admitting women took even longer, mind you). The vicar and parson were central to the social and educational life of most communities. But at the same time, Nonconformists vied with evangelicals and atheists as the extremes against which the broad church struggled to define itself. Faith was a battleground. Students argued fiercely about religion; there were anti-Catholic riots; books were burned. The newspapers fizzed with accusations and counteraccusations about the Oxford Movement, the claims of science, the discoveries of biblical archaeology. . . . Religion mattered in a way most of modern Britain has quite forgotten—though there are many places in the world that do still understand such a passionate engagement. Particularly in the middle of the nineteenth century, it really was important to be earnest about religion: it was a sign of who you were and who you wanted to be. It is easy to forget that the rational, scientific, modern novelist George Eliot was a renegade evangelical Christian, who lost her piety and her reputation, in search of her new self.

In the mind of the common-or-garden Anglican, pilgrimage in the sense that Egeria or Prudentius understood it was dangerously connected to the Catholic Church. It was the sort of thing people on the Continent did. It was associated with priests leading processions, with ritual, and, above all, with relics. Protestants dismissed relics as a besotting sin of Catholic error. Protestant truth rejected kissing old bones and didn't believe in miracles effected by touching a dead human's remains. It seemed superstitious at best, and at worst positively perverted. With the invention of the steamship and the opening of the borders of the Ottoman Empire, more and more British and American travelers visited Jerusalem. Each trip inevitably took on the aspect of a pilgrimage, but almost every Protestant was shocked not just by the small size, dirt, and, well, foreignness of the squalid Ottoman backwater, but also by the forms of worship they saw in the Church of the Holy Sepulchre. "Fetish adoration," "the worship of wood and stone," were typical accusations. One phrase was especially insulting and it was repeated and challenged, again and again. It was coined by the celebrated American archaeologist Edward Robinson, one of the pioneers of exploring the Holy Land. "Credulous superstition and pious fraud," he commented on the scene of emotional pilgrims at the site of the Crucifixion, and the words "pious fraud," with their implication of hypocrisy or deception, summed up Protestant distaste for pilgrimage when it involved the full gamut of Catholic worship.

So proper Englishmen did not go on pilgrimages, if it meant struggling toward Santiago de Compostela to kneel before the bones of Saint James. They might take their guidebook and go with Thomas Cook to observe the rituals, then write home about the exoticism and distastefulness of what they had seen. But stones and bones were not meant to be kissed. The nineteenth century is the great era for travel books, for adventure stories, for exploration, for patrolling the empire's boundaries, but especially in comparison with the medieval period, with which so much Victorian art, history writing, and literature was fascinated, pilgrimage had the air of joining a nasty cult. Even in England itself, where there had been a popular tradition of pilgrimage—Walsingham, Becket's tomb at Canterbury, Lindisfarne—when Victorian gentlemen and ladies visited churches, it was more likely to be to explore the architecture with art-historical eyes, their spiritual guide, the art critic Ruskin.

Yet pilgrimage remained a powerful lure for the English and American Protestants, in a displaced way, as it were. Thomas Carlyle was perhaps the most charismatic of Victorian sages—the grumpy and fierce intellectual was one of the most widely read and widely influential figures of the period—and he captures the drive behind this nineteenth-century pilgrim experience well when he writes, "Literature is but a branch of Religion, and always participates in its character: however, in our time, it is the only branch that still shows any greenness; and, as some think, must one day become the main stem." For Carlyle, literature these days—"in our time," as the Victorians, ever aware of themselves as living in a new age of progress, kept repeating—is starting to become a sort of religion. Cardinal Newman—now a full-blown saint—whose conversion to Catholicism was so shocking for midcentury society, typically wanted to narrow the force of literature to religious poetry: "The taste for poetry of a religious kind has in modern times in a certain sense taken the place of the deep contemplative spirit of the early Church. . . . Poetry . . . is our mysticism."

John Keble, the austere theologian who gave his name to the ugliest college in Oxford, wrote one of the most successful books of poetry, religious or otherwise, in the nineteenth century. *The Christian Year* sold a quarter of a million copies, though it is scarcely read even by scholars these days. It offers a spiritually uplifting and, to modern tastes like mine, a dull and squirmingly pious poem for every significant festive day of the year. Keble saw poetry as a sort of balm, a miracle cure for humans: the "glorious art of poetry is a kind of medicine divinely bestowed upon man," bringing "healing relief to secret mental emotion." No need, then, when in anxiety or pain, to collapse before the shrine of a saint: read a poem in the garden or by the fire. Poetry was experienced as a religion. Here's how a novelist in the 1880s captures the feeling: "Wordsworth unconsciously did for me what every religious reformer had done,—he recreated my Supreme Divinity, substituting a new and living spirit for the old deity, once alive but gradually hardened into an idol." Literature was not just medicine for the sick soul, it was inspirational, transformative, a journey of self-discovery.

This changing status of literature was made possible by technological advances in publishing and transport. Thanks to cheap paper, printing machines, the postal system, and the railway network, inexpensive copies of novels, tracts, and poems, along with newspapers, journals, and reviews, circulated swiftly across Europe and America. A whole new reading public had emerged—public education had also expanded considerably (if slowly and contentiously)—and there were fortunes to be made by publishers and writers. Where very successful books in the eighteenth century had circulated in thousands, in the nineteenth century hundreds of thousands of copies of hot, new novels flooded the market and were eagerly devoured. One consequence of this media revolution is that writers became superstars. Novelists such as Dickens or Thackeray, poets such as Tennyson, historians such as Macaulay or George Grote, essayists like Carlyle, Matthew Arnold, or Ralph Waldo Emerson, were lionized in London and New York, made tours in England and America, where thousands bought tickets to hear them lecture, and, perhaps most importantly, became figures of the imagination. To be a writer became a career choice, tinged with Romantic ideals; the image of the lady novelist, for example, or the man of letters, became the subject of hopeful aspiration, parodic jokes, and cultural prestige. As literature became religion, the writer became the sage, the prophet, the inspirational preacher and leader—the guide to one's internal life.

It is not by chance, then, that in the nineteenth century we find a new phenomenon: the tour to visit writers' houses. The birthplace, the grave, the house where the writer lived, or even where the writer was now living—all, for the first time, became sites of pilgrimage. The journey was treated like a visit to a saint's shrine. So a young man, living "'mid the din of towns and cities," in the grime and noise of the industrialized urban sprawl, might carefully plan his train trip to the north to visit Wordsworth's cottage. He would walk up from the station, noting the places and country sights memorialized by the poetry he knew and loved, and pause by the gate of the home of the master. If he was lucky, the elderly Wordsworth might give him a tour—Wordsworth did this a great deal, and had a good script. If he were too shy or polite to enter, or if Wordsworth was not there, he might pluck a leaf from the garden and jealously keep it to be pressed, and contemplated, when back again at home, in the "lonely rooms" of the town, a relic of his restorative journey back to nature, in search of the poet of nature. (I should probably say that this rather sappy composite picture is based on a set of Victorian letters about precisely such a trip and its preserved leaf. But it wasn't just sad young men— Elizabeth Barrett Browning and George Eliot too both asked for petals from the poet's garden.) To visit the writer's house was to be touched by the writer's charisma, an experience to be treasured.

The novels and poems of the nineteenth century seemed to encourage this sort of response. The description of domestic interiors is a regular set piece of Victorian fiction. When Margaret, the heroine of Mrs. Gaskell's *North and South*, enters the Thornton drawing room, she is given a moment to look around. "It seemed as though no one had been in it since the day when the furniture was bagged up with as much care as if the house was to be overwhelmed with lava, and discovered a thousand years hence. The walls were pink and gold: the patterns on the carpet represented bunches of flowers on a light ground, but it was carefully covered up in the centre by a linen drug-get, glazed and colourless." Margaret's eyes continue remorselessly to itemize the tastelessness of the room. The description concludes, "The whole room had a painfully spotted, spangled, speckled look about it, which impressed Margaret so unpleasantly that she was hardly conscious of the peculiar cleanliness required to keep everything so white and pure in such an atmosphere, or the trouble that must be willingly expended to secure the effect of icy, snowy discomfort." Cleanliness may be next to godliness, but in this room cleanliness is an icy rejection of life and comfort; the decoration is there to be preserved as decoration, rather than enjoyed as beauty. It is not hard to predict that Margaret's encounter with Mrs. Thornton is not going to be a success, and that there is something very wrong with the moral and spiritual life of a woman who could design such a space. Domestic space not only reveals the character of those who live in it and design it, but also has a powerful psychological effect on its inhabitants. Dark and gloomy houses make dark and gloomy people, or so the logic of the fiction always runs, and a warm and comforting scene will make people into warm and comfortable personalities.

This is doubly true of the natural landscape, thanks especially to the influence of the Romantic poets and novelists and their love of the natural world. Wordsworth writes beautifully of his early life amid the hills and lakes of Cumbria, as he recalls

> what I was, when first
> I came among these hills, when like a roe
> I bounded o'er the mountains by the sides
> Of the deep rivers and the lonely streams
> Wherever nature led, more like a man
> Flying from something that he dreads than one
> Who sought the thing he loved. For nature then
> (The coarser pleasures of my boyish days
> And their glad animal movements all gone by)
> To me was all in all.

The landscape had a profound influence on Wordsworth, it made him who he came to be. So authors were formed by their environment—think of how the Brontës are associated with the moors of Yorkshire—and the depiction of a place in a novel or a poem could change the place forever for its readers. When Richard Blackmoor wrote the best-selling *Lorna Doone*, with its wonderful and haunting descriptions of Exmoor, Exmoor was redubbed "Lorna Doone Country," as pilgrims visited it to rediscover the landscape of the novel on the ground. Like military historians tracing where each battalion fought on a battle-field, readers now followed Walter Scott's heroes through the Scottish Borders, or Dickens's Oliver Twist through the streets of London. Since the home and the countryside had such a formative influence on the character of a person, to visit the house and the environment of a writer was to catch a glimpse of where the writer and the stories came from, how they came into being. And since those stories and poems had such a formative effect on the reader's internal life, visiting the writer's house felt like a journey of self-discovery too.

So walking to a poet's cottage or a novelist's stately home could never be just a day out. In fact—and a book about pilgrimage is a good place to reveal this—there is a small but flourishing academic field known as the history of walking. Walking, say its historians, was invented at the end of the eighteenth century and became a real fad in the nineteenth—a Romantic invention and Victorian hobby. Now, obviously, "walking" here means walking out of choice, as a pastime—"pedestrian travel." The first use of the term "pedestrian" in this sense is attributed by the *Oxford English Dictionary* to Wordsworth, significantly enough, who made tramping the hills a mode of spiritual transformation—to "pant slow up the endless Alp of life," as he put it memorably, if rather painfully. At one time, walking was an unmistakable index of poverty (it may still be in parts of the United States where the automobile is king). Long-distance walking was associated with vagrancy—the tramp, the beggar, the bum. But through the Romantic era and into the Victorian period, as men (and some women) took up walking as a pastime, it came also to be associated with the mobility of the radical mind. The walking trip across Europe, exposing yourself to new cultures, thoughts, people, removed you from the parochial, the conservative, the narrow-minded. (It is an area too of inbuilt gender difference: very few women indeed made the sorts of trips that were so important for, say, Wordsworth or Robert Louis Stevenson.) It is fascinating to see how often the radical, literary, heroic walker has a significant encounter with a vagrant or beggar. Real walkers need to distinguish themselves from economic walkers, even if they learned some lesson from them too.

Writing about such trips became significant explorations of self-formation and helped make walking fashionable for others, especially hopeful writers. So the young Keats went for his walking tour of the Lakes specifically to get "such an accumulation of stupendous recol-lolections" in preparation for his vocation as a poet (the misspelling is no doubt part of the enthusiasm of youth for the adventure to come): "I will clamber through the clouds and exist." Not only were dozens of walking tour books produced, but also essays about the principle and theory of walking. William Hazlitt's is one of the first and most delightful: "Give me the clear blue sky over my head, and the green turf beneath my feet, a winding road before me, and a three hours' march to dinner—and then to thinking!" The trip to the writer's house also took on the full weight of this new notion of walking: getting there was as important a process as the visit itself. So at the turn of the nineteenth century, the poet Samuel Taylor Coleridge went on a tour with his friend John Hucks: "Behold us, then, more like two pilgrims performing a journey to the tomb of some wonder-working saint, than men travelling for the pleasure and amusement." The walk to the house of the writer itself became invested with the significance of a pilgrimage.

I must admit, my excitement at my editor's suggestion that I "do something Victorian" could not repress one note of surprise. When I have lectured and taught in America, I have noticed a huge difference between American and British responses to the Victorian. British students, especially for me at Cambridge, do their studying surrounded by Victorian buildings, statues, books. I myself had been taught by teachers brimming with anecdotes of their own teachers, who had actually been Victorians. My grandfathers had grown up "'mid the din of towns and cities" at the end of the Victorian era, and I had seen the East End streets in London and the docks of Liverpool where they had roamed. On my office walls, I have paintings by the Bloomsbury group, the wild children and snide debunkers of their Victorian parents, and from my window I see every day the path where A. E. Housman walked, writing his poems in his head. For most of the American students I have taught in the United States, this sense of physical and personal continuity just isn't there with the same intensity. There was no Victorian era in Sacramento. The Civil War, cowboys and the West, the gold rush, were hugely evocative and powerful icons of the nineteenth century. But outside the bustling university departments of nineteenth-century studies, the adjective "Victorian" was less likely to go to the heart of an American cultural identity. For the British, still obsessed with class and working through the end of empire (nostalgically, painfully, apologetically, reflectively . . .), or for those of my generation, for whom the memory of Margaret Thatcher demanding a return to Victorian values is still vivid, a Victorian pilgrimage can still be a journey of self-discovery. So much about us was put in place either by our Victorian ancestors or in direct reaction to them.

It turns out, however, that the pilgrimage to Victorian writers' houses has been an American fixation too. In the nineteenth century, English literature—English culture in general—loomed over the development of American writing and thinking. Much of what Americans read in the nineteenth century was written in Britain (often in pirated editions, as there was no international copyright agreement yet). Many British authors, like Charles Dickens and Matthew Arnold and Charles Kingsley, were treated as celebrities when they toured the States, and whole communities turned out to hear dramatic recitals from the novels or lectures on cultural matters. The development of a particular American literary culture still looked nervously and brashly and proudly toward Europe, and Britain in particular. So Mark Twain's *A Connecticut Yankee in King Arthur's Court* hilariously plays off the difference between the old country and the new, and Henry James, who lived the last forty years of his life in England, epitomizes both a longing for and an alienation from a culture that could not be found in America—an earlier model for Hemingway in Spain or Gershwin's American in Paris. The elite of American society traveled widely in Europe, the more so as American wealth and influence grew. This special relationship between the United States and Britain frames American tourism to England. For Americans, a trip to England meant a complex engagement with cultural heritage as well as an encounter with the British Empire at its height. In fact, my journeying was going to follow some celebrated and sophisticated American travelers. Washington Irving visited Sir Walter Scott in 1816 in his house at Abbotsford (and that is my first port of call); Ralph Waldo Emerson visited Wordsworth's house in the Lake District, our second destination. Mark Twain was one of many writers who went to Stratford-upon-Avon, to see the house of Shakespeare and, more bathetically, as he himself recognized through gritted teeth, to take tea at the house of Marie Corelli, the very much still alive and embarrassingly vulgar novelist. Stratford too will be on our itinerary. And when it comes to Freud's house, for a host of New Yorkers, that couch is very much part of the interior decoration of the mind.

The cliché of the rich American tourist oblivious to or baffled by the niceties of British society starts in the nineteenth century, and there are plenty of snide stories, especially from its last decades, about crass groups of badly dressed Yankees buying fake antiques and eating with the wrong fork. In part, this is just English snobbery and self-regard (familiar today too), but the nineteenth century also invented the idea of the tourist as a sort of poor quality traveler. Thomas Cook and the package holiday get going at this time (their first trips were to English stately homes by train), and immediately the counterimage of the Real Traveler emerges. Real travelers, the myth goes, have real experiences in real contact with the communities they visit; tourists merely gawp, follow the beaten track, and snap photos. *We* are travelers, *they* are tourists. Americans make jokes about (American) tourists too. Mark Twain's letters home from his trip to the Holy Land, published first in a newspaper in New York, then as the book *Innocents Abroad*, set the tone: amused, sly, wry, distanced from the crowd, the writer nonetheless goes to the same places as the companions he mocks. A pilgrimage, even though the word seems to announce its own seriousness, needs the right attitude. It has to be an antitourist trail, even and especially when going to tourist spots.

Washington Irving, Mark Twain, and Ralph Waldo Emerson were no innocents abroad, and no one was more sensitive to the nuances of cultural interaction than Henry James, an exile whose novels repeatedly dissect the appearance of innocence. Their pilgrimages were not casual excursions. Visiting writers' houses was for them—and still is for all of us—a moment when we come face to face, not with the cuteness of Olde England, but with a sense of cultural heritage. What do writers and their works mean to us? How do places form us as people? How do we look at the past?

My reflections were beginning to melt my wife's scorn. Washington Irving and Mark Twain were clearly better models than the dumb American sidekick. She might, she confessed, be one of my four Jews on a train. (By this stage, the negotiation felt as tense and drawn out as a Victorian marriage proposal.) The plan was to journey as much as possible by Victorian means and following Victorian guidebooks. That meant trains and walking. A bus could replace cart or horse where absolutely necessary, but no cars and no planes. Like so many characters in Victorian stories, we would consult the train timetable, wear stout shoes, and stay in the local inn. The journey was an essential part of the pilgrimage and could not be rushed. There would be five destinations: first, Abbotsford, Sir Walter Scott's baronial pile in the Scottish borders, the earliest of the houses to enter the public imagination, and the furthest from home; then down to Dove Cottage and Rydal Mount, Wordsworth's houses in the Lake District; third, across the Pennines to Haworth and the Brontë parsonage; then, more surprisingly, to Shakespeare' s house in Stratford—of course, Shakespeare isn't a Victorian writer, but his house was discovered and rebuilt as a national monument in the Victorian era, a testament to the importance of the National Poet for the country. Finally, we would return to London and to Freud's house in Hampstead. Freud made his consulting room there in 1938, an exact replica of his nineteenth-century study in Vienna. If there is any figure who marks the transition from Victorian society to modernity, it is Freud. The journey would thus go from the heroes of the Romantic movement at the beginning of the century to the great redrafter of family romance at its end.

Each of these houses fired the imagination of its visitors. Each was taken as a fundamental expression of the writer and the writer's creative works: to visit them was not just an act of curiosity but to uncover an insight into the writer's self, a sign of the writer's self-expression, and to experience an encounter of serious significance for the visitor's self. Each house was a site of pilgrimage, and each is now swathed in stories about those encounters: and as Chaucer knew, any decent pilgrimage needs its storytelling.

But as we prepared to set out with our friends, David and Helen (I was particularly relying on David, a doctor with Schopenhauerian tendencies, to provide the depressive notes, as well as the medical backup that all good Jewish trips build in), I found myself still slightly anxious. I had read many books by now on pilgrimage, on writers' houses, on these writers and their houses, and many, many words by the writers whose houses we would be visiting. But I still felt none of the passionate connection to objects and places that a genuine biographer should feel in his bones. I love books, need books, but I have little interest in authors and their things. I cannot see why I should go and look at John Updike's typewriter, or Saul Bellow's apartment, or Salman Rushdie's trousers. I'd rather read their books. I have never visited a grave, at least not the grave of anyone famous. I have looked at autographs without breaking down; I have stood where Caesar was assassinated and where Pericles spoke to the Athenian democracy, without the need to orate or shout "Et tu Brute" (which Caesar didn't say, anyway). I find it hard to credit that *Harry Potter* is indebted to the particular coffee shop that J. K. Rowling sat in, or that the trademark triviality of Jeffrey Archer's prose should be laid at the door of Grantchester and its beautiful vicarage. As I came across stories of people weeping uncontrollably at the sight of Freud's couch, I became more and more baffled by the phenomenon I was about to trace. Was there something wrong with me that I couldn't feel the emotional pull of a writer's detritus? For me, books opened a world of the imagination, a world in the mind: why would you want to shut the door on such a greater landscape to fixate on some merely real place or object? Would looking at the Brontë parsonage or Shakespeare's birthplace really get me closer to the literature I cherished? I felt I had a lot to learn about why so many people, both sophisticated thinkers and bored tour parties on a wet Sunday, want to visit writers' houses. Like all pilgrims, I was setting out on a search for something, a search I rather feared would be about my own desires and blindness, my own intellectual and emotional investments.

2

LION HUNTING IN SCOTLAND

I T IS HARD NOW to imagine a world without celebrity. Not only are the TV channels and newspapers dominated by grinning and weeping faces desperate for their fifteen minutes of fame, but also, thanks to advertising and the media world, serious authors and musicians and artists are locked into the same economics of culture. Almost every month, without any apparent irony (though with plenty of cynicism, I expect), another journalist regrets that children today want to be famous, but have no idea what they want to be famous for—as if the magazines and newspapers that print such articles were not deeply complicit with what they publicly deplore. We are meant to know who is on the A list of celebs, who is merely B list (the sub-B divisions are mentioned only with a sigh or a sneer), and we also know how such stars of publicity are meant to behave. "The celebrity" is a modern cultural myth: there is a whole set of expectations—from outrageous egos, to demands for special treatment, to divorce and sexual license—that everyone, stars and audiences and commentators, loves to see fulfilled. Celebrity has become one of the stories by which our world is organized, our own normality defined.

It wasn't always so. (Like walking, celebrity has a history.) The pursuit of fame in some sense has, of course, always been with us, even in a Christian culture that made humbleness a virtue. The very first work of Western literature, Homer's *Iliad*, full of thoroughly un-Christian boasting and violence, takes as its premise that its angry hero, Achilles, is willing to give up his life for immortal glory. The pursuit of everlasting fame motivates many an epic and many an epic life. Alexander the Great traveled on his expeditions of world conquest with a copy of the *Iliad* under his pillow, as he tried to live up to Achilles as his role model. And he built a string of cities called Alexandria to perpetuate his renown. Lots of love poets, like Ovid, promised their lover's name would live forever (if only she would sleep with a poor artist: the original kiss and tell . . .).

But modern celebrity, which allows one, finally, to be famous for being famous, looks like a different thing from Alexander's pursuit of military dominance of the world and his program of city foundation. Modern celebrity cannot really work without modern media and their speed of dissemination and penetration of the market. It was the nineteenth century that invented the new technology that made this explosion possible, and it is in the nineteenth century too that we see the new cult of celebrity beginning to flourish into its modern form.

But it is still a strange thought, for me at least, that one of the key figures in this invention of celebrity was a dumpy Scottish poet with a limp who had trained as a lawyer and had a thing for old Scottish traditions—Sir Walter Scott. But he was one of the first artists to be treated to the full glare of the modern style of fame. I must confess that I have never much cared for Scott's poetry. "Oh, what a tangled web we weave, when first we practise to deceive!" are the only lines to have stuck in my mind (they are quoted often enough, though not many people actually know they were written by Scott, let alone in *Marmion*). His poetry hit just the right note at the beginning of the nineteenth century, and I don't get on with it for exactly the reasons that made it so popular then. He was intent, like an archaeologist, to dig up the old and lost world of bards and minstrels, singing around the fire in the laird's hall, songs about romantic ladies pining and swooning and chivalric heroes—sheep stealers—nobly pursuing vengeance. He was fascinated by the olden times of Scotland: *Marmion* is an epic about the sixteenth-century battle of Flodden Field, where an invading Scottish army was trounced by the English. The poetry itself tries to sound like old-style ballads from those days, but I can't help wishing for something a little less like a Hallmark card ("The last of all the Bards was he, Who sung of border chivalry; For, welladay!, their date was fled, His tuneful brethren all were dead . . ."). What is more, both the romance and the epic are in service of a nationalism that is typical of the artistic and political inspiration of the nineteenth century: nationalism needed to discover the fertile past, the soil from which the modern nation had grown—our nation's history. All this makes me quite jumpy, as I catch myself remembering that nationalism as an ideology bore much sick fruit, that we don't do romance like that anymore, and sheep-stealing doesn't exactly have a real heroic tinge. Not reveling in Scott's poetry is one way I recognize how far I am from the era when it was such a hit.

Scott's poetry made him famous, as poetry could in the nineteenth century. But his novels made him a celebrity. He turned to fiction writing because he needed some cash, and so in 1814 he wrote *Waverley*. This was the first of what would come to be known as "the Waverley novels," a series of historical fictions, mainly set around the borders of Scotland—of which the most famous, *Ivanhoe*, *Rob Roy*, *The Bride of Lammermoor*, and *The Heart of Midlothian*, have titles that remain instantly recognizable, even if the books themselves are not as much read as once they were. Although there had been plenty of widely read novels from the eighteenth century onward, the genre still had an image problem. The novel was seen as a slightly louche, if not seamy, form—a book to be read with one hand, was Rousseau's definition. Scott made historical fiction a genre that anyone could read, and seriously.

This reputation of unseemliness might help explain why *Waverley* was published anonymously. But the anonymity turned out to be a masterstroke of publicity. *Waverley* was a magnificent success, read by thousands across Europe and America, with fervor and excitement. Subsequent volumes in the series were also published anonymously under the new brand of "the Author of *Waverley*," and as the new books were eagerly waited for—with *Harry Potter*-like queues and guesswork about future plots—the identity of the author became a feverish question. Famous authors and politicians wrote in praise; they sent their letters to the publisher and received replies, written by the Author of *Waverley*, but under the name of the publisher. Rumors about his identity spread and kept the public fascinated. This ruse lasted till 1827 (by which time it was an open secret in all the right circles: already in 1815 Scott had taken tea with George, the Prince Regent, who had wished to meet the Author of *Waverley*). Reading Scott became a sign of a certain cultural life. Men as well as women confessed to losing themselves in the stories; families read the books together; the characters became touchstones; the view of history offered by Scott formed the imagination of a generation. After Scott, the novel became the powerhouse of nineteenth-century culture, the genre by which we know the Victorian era.

The Author of *Waverley* became a literary celebrity of a sort the world had not seen before. The only other writer to touch him was the poet Byron. Byron published the first part of "Childe Harold's Pilgrimage" in 1812 and, as he put it, "awoke one morning and found himself famous." Byron had the advantage of a wild and too-public sex life, and, soon, a young death pursuing the classic Romantic dream of fighting for the liberation of Greece from the tyranny of the Ottoman Empire. He set the model for the James Deans and Kurt Cobains of modern culture (though with a touch more class—he was *Lord* Byron—not to mention a touch more articulacy). At John Murray's, his publisher, there is an archive of "fan mail," mostly from women he had never met, emoting about how his poetry had changed their lives, their *internal* lives. (One shouldn't underestimate how much emotional turmoil it demonstrated for a woman within the bounds of nineteenth-century propriety to write a letter expressing such feelings to a stranger.) Even the *Edinburgh Review*, not given to slushiness, reflected that readers felt Byron's poetry "as secrets whispered to chosen ears": "We feel as if chosen out from a crowd of lovers."

As writers became celebrities, a new vocabulary fell into shape. The artist of the moment was a "literary lion," and the hero of culture was "lionized." The term actually came about because there was a famous little zoo at the Tower of London that had lions as its main attraction: visiting the lions was the archetypal tourist outing. So when the literary celebrity entered London life, he became the social equivalent of a trip to the zoo and was pursued by "lion hunters," the men and women who loved to glow in the reflected glory of being seen with such artists, such molders of the soul. (The lions at the Tower were a bit mangy, but so, frankly, were some of the literary types.) There were articles in popular magazines like *Punch* about "lion hunting," and guidebooks appeared, called *London Lions for Country Cousins and Friends about Town*, or *New Guide to the 'Lions' of London*. Charlotte Brontë, who was pathologically uncomfortable with strangers, describes her misery at being taken up for a three-day trip by Sir James and Lady Kay-Shuttleworth, the doyens of upper-crust lionizers: "I wish it was well over," she writes dismally on the first day. Even Byron was disconcerted when he "found the room full of strangers who had come to stare at me as at some outlandish beast in a rareeshow." Charles Dickens, finger as ever on the pulse of popular humor, conjures, in *Pickwick Papers*, a brilliant caricature of an aspiring social climber, desperate for a literary salon of her own. Her name? Mrs. Leo Hunter.

I felt I had to explain something about Scott, his fame, and his importance in the history of the novel because my wife, like the rest of my family, hadn't read any of his novels and asked rather too often why we were going all the way to Scotland, and what was the name of his house, again. Wordsworth, Brontë, Shakespeare were up there in the pantheon, and Freud was king of New York—but Walter Scott? She knew that I had bought the full set of the Waverley novels, going cheap, in a pretentious adolescent moment, and had traipsed them, unopened, around our various apartments and houses, always stacked on the top shelf. But in the last few years, now that I had added Victorian studies to my classical credentials, I had read a good selection—and had actually loved them. *Waverley*, to my surprise, was not just a totally gripping historical tale but extraordinarily sophisticated, witty, and, well, *modern*. Scott puts the preface on the last page, on the grounds that readers always turn to the last page first and never read prefaces—so if he puts his preface at the end, there is some chance readers will read it at the right moment. *The Antiquary*, my favorite and Scott's too, is a wonderful, tongue-in-cheek parody of the fantasies of historical fiction—Scott's own obsessions. I had spent a day in a deck chair in the sun in the Fellows' Garden at King's College reading it with total joy. If this is work, give me more. . . . So I enthused. It made no difference. Scott remained a closed book for her. The fact that he had been a lawyer made it worse. "I don't even have time to *read* fiction," she exploded, as I interrupted the usual crisis of preparing for court the next morning. I didn't think this was the right moment to explore the relation between fiction and a divorce client's statement.

Celebrity doesn't guarantee lasting fame. Scott began to be sniffed at by highbrow critics, went out of fashion before the end of the nineteenth century, and by the middle of the twentieth was the epitome of the uncool—the sort of book that was given as a school prize or as a present by an unloved relative. So no surprise that, out of all our destinations, my fellow pilgrims disdained Scott. Not even the blockbuster film of *Ivanhoe* in 1952 (or the TV show in 1982) made much of a dent. (Jews read *Ivanhoe*, though, because it stars a beautiful Jewish heroine, who ends up in the equivalent of a nunnery, because she clearly couldn't get married—too Jewish—or killed—not right for a beautiful heroine—the only alternative endings available.) But Scott's house, Abbotsford, is the perfect place to start our pilgrimage, and not just because Scott is the earliest of the nineteenth-century authors we will be following, and not just because—I found myself almost wagging my figure at the nonbelievers—he is so important in the history of the novel and of writers' celebrity. The house itself justifies the trip.

Unlike all the other writers' houses on our itinerary, Abbotsford was designed and built by the author as an expression of himself: it was constructed to embody architecturally what "Scott" meant in the world, and was created as a shrine to himself as author. Scott claimed to have seen the site as a youngster and longed to live there. It was called, with Scottish bluntness, Clarty Hole (roughly translated, "shitty dump"), but for his baronial and chivalric aspirations Abbotsford seemed a more suitable moniker, with just the right touch of re-

CHAPTER TWO

22

ligious history and old-style grandeur. He bought the cottage and the land for an inflated price in 1812 as a sign of his arrival as a poet, and proceeded to lavish a huge amount of money building the house of his dreams—with all the fantasy and vigor of a Randolph Hearst or Michael Jackson. Every detail was organized; the grounds were planted out with intense seriousness; tours were conducted with embracing commentary by the master and owner himself. It was one of the first modern houses to have multiple guidebooks and articles written about it. The press oohed and aahed over the costs, each article suggesting a larger total expenditure. (And it *was* a hugely expensive enterprise.) Kind visitors and hagiographic guidebooks called it "a monument of the high historical imagination." Ruskin, with his discerning eye, called it "perhaps the most incongruous pile that gentlemanly modernism ever designed." For Washington Irving, "a little realm of romance was suddenly opened before me."

For me, Ruskin's description was the most immediately alluring invitation. How could one not want to see "the most incongruous pile" of all the incongruities of Victorian architectural folly, especially in the name of "gentlemanly modernism"—a delightfully snide recognition of Scott's peculiarity? But Abbotsford also raises the central questions of writers and their houses in an especially sharp manner. The power of Scott over the imagination of readers across the world prompted a fascination with the man himself: there are several major biographies, starting with the seven-volume life (stretching to ten volumes in the second edition) by his son-in-law, John Lockhart. Lockhart was something of a prodigy: he graduated with a first-class degree in classics from Oxford at the age of only seventeen; he was the lead reviewer of *Blackwood's*, the leading, staunchly Tory journal; he went on to edit the trendsetting *Quarterly Review*; and he even killed a rival critic in a duel. His biography of Scott has been called the second greatest biography in English (after Boswell on Johnson, of course), and one might have thought that such a masterpiece would have deterred rivals. But many others, it seems, felt the need to try to capture the wellsprings of Scott's genius. In Hollywood terms, his life is actually extremely dull: he wrote books, and, despite his success, was financially crippled by a ludicrously poor business investment, which meant he had to write more books. All the biographies I have read set out primarily to find what made Scott tick as a writer, how he achieved such a hold over his audience. Scott seems to play up to this: look at my house, he seems to say, and see me in my home, my space as a writer, my place of inspiration. This is where the Waverley novels were written. Here, at Abbotsford, you will find Scott.

I don't know. Can you build a house to reveal your inner self? Or is it just the projection of an image—acknowledging and manipulating your readers' hope of finding the real man? What sort of display did Scott think Abbotsford made? In his writing, he is so guarded and canny about self-revelation, always hiding behind a grin and a twist of disingenuous self-mockery. When he invited Washington Irving in to see his daughter sing Scottish ballads by the fire, how knowing was his picture of "the Scott family at home"? Was this the *People* or *Hello* magazine of its time? Scott seems to have been both deeply serious about Abbotsford as a venture and wryly self-conscious about his public persona at the same time.

That's why I thought the first stage of our journey should be to Abbotsford. I wanted to test the principle of the pilgrimage from the start. If writers' houses do get us in touch with the writer and his work, as I keep being told, what happens when the writer constructs his house like a stage set on which to act the role of author? Will it make a difference that this is not a romantically humble garret or cottage or parsonage, but a baronial castle with turrets and a huge driveway? I am afraid it might prove easier to feel warmly attached to poor Charlotte Brontë writing at the kitchen table than to Sir Walter Scott, Bart., surrounded by suits of armor, famous guests, and the trappings of Victorian status. Scott put up his Latin motto over the door at Abbotsford: *clausus tutus ero*, which we can translate as "I'll be safe behind walls," or "security in concealment." The Latin is also an anagram of "UUalterus Scotus," or . . . Walter Scott. He conceals and reveals himself in or behind the words he blazons over the entrance, words that promise safety when the boundaries are kept in place. That seems to catch the problem perfectly.

The train from King's Cross to Edinburgh takes you gradually north, through the postindustrial wastelands of the midlands to the preindustrial wastelands of the borders, as the terrain changes to rolling hills and then mountains, and the houses from concrete to brick to old gray stone. The journey gives you time to acclimatize to another country without getting up from your seat, a swift lesson in geography and the class history of north and south, through the windows' images, slowly transforming as they flash past. No shuffling security lines, no desultory strolling round garishly lit shops, no forms to fill out, no instant transfer from lounge to foreignness. You can sit opposite each other all the way and chat, face to face. Trains are much better than planes for people-watching too. Our cast included a blond, straight-haired American family, with pampered complexions and more luggage than they could possibly carry, failing to galvanize a surly English porter with their friendliness; a nervously proud mother taking her confident daughter to look around universities; two silent government officials, tapping away at mysterious documents on their laptops, a can of lager every two hours; and two elderly couples, all dressed for a cold summer, with thin sandwiches in Tupperware boxes, delighted to meet each other and exchange stories of the fangledness, new or otherwise, of contemporary life. And four Jews, talking too loudly, and eating a gastro-picnic with overexpressive gusto.

The pilgrimage, however, nearly foundered as soon as we got to Edinburgh. I had hoped to do the whole journey by Victorian transport, by slow travel. But to get from Edinburgh to Abbotsford—a journey of some thirty-five miles—is really difficult these days if you don't just jump in a car and pop down the A7. The train service that once ran to Galashiels was cut by the Tory government of the 1960s, though in places you can still see the tracks, one of the many scars of planning policy across the country. It would have to be a bus (or two days' walking or a whole day biking, neither of which thrilled the room-service mavens I had chosen to travel with). The bus would get us to Galashiels or Melrose, but that still left a few miles. A bike had seemed the obvious solution when planning the trip at home. But "I canna take the bike on the bus." "Why?" "Against the rules." "But you take push chairs!" "Aye. But I canna take a bike." "There is plenty of room and I will buy a ticket for my bike." "I canna take a bike." In the bathroom of the bus station there was a sign, hand-written in rough capital letters on a white paper bag and stuck with Blu-Tack on the door of the cubicle. "Sorry about the bulb. It will get changed sometime." To my jaundiced eye, it seemed grimly symbolic of Scottish infrastructure.

Yet even before leaving Edinburgh, Scott is there, a celebrity. You arrive at Waverley Station, named in 1846 for the novels, and as you walk up onto Princes Street, toward the buses, the first monument you see is Scott's Monument. This is a gothic tower, elaborately pinnacled and stained-glass windowed, in the dirtiest red-gray sandstone, built on his death by public demand to proclaim Scott's importance. It is just over two hundred feet tall, and you can climb its spiral staircases, squeezing past anyone coming down, to a series of small viewing terraces, which give a stupendous view of the wondrous architecture of Edinburgh: those beetling Georgian tenements, huge domestic fortresses like cliff faces, larger than the castle itself, and the hills and the Firth of Forth beyond. Scott himself, with his dog, is portrayed in a heroic funerary statue at the foot of the monument. So, you get into New York, and arrive not at Grand Central but at Portnoy Station, and walk down Forty-second Street into Times Square to see a huge statue and monument to Philip Roth (designed by Andy Warhol). Dream on. Modern culture may make writers famous, but this sort of public recognition of their importance in creating the public, imaginative life of a society seems inconceivable for us today. The Victorians—bridge-builders, imperialists, industrialists—not only made celebrities of writers but also celebrated them, in life and in death.

Without bikes, the journey to Dryburgh was ignominiously completed by taxi. Dryburgh had seemed the perfect place to stay. The ruined abbey by the river Tweed was one of Scott's favorite Romantic haunts, and he was buried there. The funeral was described as "like the funeral of royalty": a long cortege, thousands crying by the roadside, speeches. The event was covered at length by all the major newspapers, and Felicia Hemans, the best-selling female poet of the period—who also coined the phrase "stately homes"—wrote a long poem called "The Funeral Day of Sir Walter Scott," which mourned "the kingly ruler in the realms of mind," "lord of the buried past." Scott regularly took his visitors on the walk or ride to Dryburgh, and liked to talk of the beauty of the ruins in moonlight. The abbey ruins were shutting when we arrived, the only visitors. "You canna gae in." "Not for a minute?" "You canna gae in." "Over the wall from our hotel?"—the wall was easily climbable—"You'd better not!"

I needed to clear my head—pilgrims are often flattened by the trivial, dismal contingencies of the road in the search for something grander, I tried to comfort myself—and set off for a walk on my own in the evening sunlight. The horses pulling the hearse with Scott's coffin had stopped, as they had so often with their master in life, on a bluff overlooking the valley a couple of miles away. Scott had stood and described the landscape there to Washington Irving. The hedgerows were full of flowers; a single deer looked up intently from a lush field of long grass; yellow chaffinches and sparrows shot through the low branches. The countryside, as Washington Irving remarked, is disappointingly unsublime—no rocky crags and cataracts—but it has rolling fields and the three Eildon hills, which dominate the landscape, and the Tweed, which curls through the woods and farms. I walked for nearly two hours and saw only one car and one person, who leaped out of his Porsche at Scott's View, glanced around, leaped back in, and roared off. The lack of city noise and city air calmed me down, and even without any people around there was no sense of emptiness. The road was one it was easy to imagine becoming rapidly familiar and loved. There was an old cottage or farmhouse every so often, the occasional oddly shaped tree; different vistas of fields and woods. I was walking the route Scott had taken repeatedly and talked many a visitor through. On a summer's evening, it was warm, benign, embracing. I could see how Scott fell in love with these surroundings and then peopled them with adventures and history and memories.

The eight miles or so to Abbotsford, a winding road by the Tweed, seemed too long to march with our bags (though it would have been a lovely cycle ride). I had read many, many descriptions of Victorian travel, but I don't think I had fully appreciated the timescale involved, until now. The ten minutes or so by cab from Dryburgh to Abbotsford represented a good morning's walk. When Edward Lear, the nonsense poet and painter, traveled in the Lake District sketching, he took a leisurely six weeks, on foot largely. For Washington Irving to visit Scott a journey of a couple of weeks needed to be planned. It isn't just that modern travel itself is faster, but that there is a different attitude toward what takes time, acceptably. I found myself getting grumpy when the taxi was five minutes late, rushing to get between towns as quickly as possible, and agreeing that a day's walk was too long and too hard just for a visit. The lengthy walk, veined with serious conversation, dotted with observation of the world around, interrupted by meetings with strangers, punctuated by unreliable hostelries, is no longer with us as a necessary and familiar part of life. Now, with headphones on to provide a soundtrack to the pseudo-movie, eyes focused on the mobile phone, from global concession coffee shop to subway, the walk to work promotes a different set of relations between humans, and between us and the world around. "You only get so many days off work," my wife reminded me firmly, in her senior partner's voice. "And it's not worth it, to go away too long: the chaos at work when you get home, the backlog." I nodded, realizing in a slightly melancholic way that one bar to understanding the Victorian pilgrimage to writers' houses was our sheer inability to take time over travel, to let the words of the poems slowly form our minds and direct our eyes, to walk toward the source of those words, to seek a conversation there.

Abbotsford certainly is a "most incongruous pile [of] gentlemanly modernism," and all the more wonderful for it. It is a large, gray, stone baronial hall, built as if modeled by the asymmetries of a long

The approach to Abbotsford: "Perhaps the most incongruous pile that gentlemanly modernism ever designed," John Ruskin.

history of development, with turrets and oddly crenelated roofs, and set in really pretty walled and porticoed gardens, hilly woodland, and flowering meadows down to the Tweed. It has become even more incongruous as the modern suburbs have stretched toward it. It is also the fullest expression of "gentlemanly modernism" that one could imagine: gentlemanly, with the full power of its early Victorian use—formed by heroic models, a medieval past, a classical education, a belief in noble standards of life and living, all embodied in a physical world of a certain luxury without ostentation and an easy assertion of the privilege of money and class. But modernist too—in that it is the most self-conscious act of self-expression and the most elaborate construction of a stage for the self, a stage made up of fragments shored against ruin. But there is a particular integrity in the constructedness: everywhere you can see the hand of Scott, his will and obsession and expression of public life. The sense of Scott *making up* Abbotsford is so strong that even those who don't come loving Scott's novels or fresh from reading Lockhart's life, will find the house a riveting place to wander through. What makes the space so compelling is a unique combination. It is, first of all, a fantasy we could all share: to build the house of our dreams. But for most of us, those dreams turn out to be rather trivial and predictable: large rooms, a swimming pool, white carpets, whatever—it's rather sad that dream homes, even or especially in soap operas or films, are rarely architectural master-pieces, or buildings genuinely to excite the imagination. Most people's heavens are equally mundane. But for Scott—and this is the second element—the dream was fueled by the specific imaginative world of a set of novels and poems, a very particular, fantastical, and shared dreamworld that also filled the minds of his readers. It is seeing Scott build *this* dreamworld that makes Abbotsford so alluring.

Take the entrance hall. It is visually overwhelming, not least be-cause for Scott, in Robert Louis Stevenson's words, "the world is so full of a number of things." Opposite the door is a carved stone fire-place, backed with blue Delft tiles. The walls are paneled, the floor laid with elaborately patterned colored stone, the ceiling hung with coats-of-arms of leading Scottish families, the windows filled with hand-painted stained glass displaying Scott's armorial bearing. There is a written inscription around the ceiling, announcing the display of the coat-of-arms. All around the walls and over the other surfaces are objects: armor, animal skulls, weapons, human skulls, statues. The ef-fect could be just one of grand, pseudo-Gothic splendor, an exuberant example of what is seen frequently, if less wholeheartedly, elsewhere, from the heyday of Victorian medievalism. But Scott is keen to tell us that the stonework of the fireplace is copied from the abbot's stall at Melrose Abbey (this is Abbotsford). So too both the eastern and western ends of the room have statues of saints copied from Melrose Abbey. The paneling itself was taken from the Auld Kirk, the church within the Old Abbey at Dunfermline. But on the eastern wall, in two niches that are modeled after niches for saints in Melrose, there are two full suits of feudal steel armor with a six-foot two-handed sword. On the western wall there are "spoils from the field of Waterloo, where I collected them in person, very shortly after that memorable action," including two French cuirasses. Scott had lunch with the Duke of

The entrance hall of Abbotsford: "A little realm of romance was suddenly opened before me," Washington Irving (1835).

Wellington at the battle site, with a full explanatory tour of the positions. There are also cannonballs from the siege of Roxburgh Castle in 1460. To add to this mixture of the religious and the military, even more bizarrely, there are, on the mantelpiece, models of the skulls of Robert the Bruce, hero of Scottish nationalism, and of Guardsman Shaw, a Life Guard who fought at Waterloo and was famous as a prizefighter. I could go on: there are many more such objects, each tagged to a site or a person, and each lovingly displayed. This is not really a "medieval style" room (the idea of the themed room, a total immersion in a past style, started a bit later, in the 1830s). It is a collection, a set of fragments of narratives, each linked to a famous moment in history or a famous building, put together is a riotous jumble, organized by the storyteller's desire, his commitment to national history, military glamour, and antiquarian fascination. The French call this sort of collection of fragments into a new story *bricolage*. Scott's house is a masterpiece of bricolage.

There is one cabinet to the right of the door that is easily missed in the richness of the display. It contains the suit of clothes that Scott wore for his last sitting for a portrait, a pair of natty black, gray and white checked trousers, a black frock coat, white leather gloves with black tracing, and a gray furry top hat, together with his ivory cane and black shoes. In the nineteenth century, you could have seen his green coat, with frayed right cuff; and, at first, the clothes he last wore just before his death. This caused some consternation. For some, it was deeply touching to see the familiar coat or traveling clothes: it brought back dear memories of a friend or admired hero. For others, especially as the century became more earnest, this display slipped over the boundary of good taste. While the chair on which the Wizard of the North had sat was treated with awe, the trousers were somehow too close to the body of the man himself. The chair was the receptacle of suitably clothed genius, the trousers housed something more fleshy. The desire to feel the intimate presence of the author was amply fulfilled without such distracting immediacy.

Every room on show in the house—only the ground floor is maintained in this way and open to visitors—is like a cabinet of curiosities. The study has the desk and black leather chair, heavily sunken with the weight of Scott's form, center stage. His glasses and still dirty blotter are there under glass. This was Scott's private space, where he worked. But there is also a chair here made with wood from the beams of Robroyston, the house where William Wallace, resistance hero of the Scottish nationalists, was captured in the fourteenth century, to be taken to his execution. David Erskine, Earl of Buchan, in the same spirit, put up a thirty-one-foot sandstone statue of Wallace on a promontory above Dryburgh in 1814, on the route from Dryburgh to Scott's View. This highly symbolic chair was transported—to the delight and celebration of thousands, we are told—by canal, with the town band playing nationalist tunes, to Abbotsford. "It is quite invaluable to me," wrote Scott. Like the skull of Bruce, this chair is a sign and symptom of Scott as national and nationalist hero, the historian of a people's past, a role he played up to. The nineteenth century was the great era for the invention of nationalism and for the invention of the traditions of the people to go along with such nationalism. Part of Scott's hold on his readers' imagination was through his tapping into this nascent political enthusiasm, and the objects with which he filled his house reflect this idealism.

The library is a particularly spectacular room, with a huge bay window and some nine thousand books. Despite the heavy plaster ceiling, painted to look like cedarwood, and based on Rosslyn Chapel (the one in *The Da Vinci Code*...), it is a light and airy space in which one would actually want to read—and it has a particularly remarkable cabinet of collected objects in it. The library is, for me at least, the most engaging room in the house, and not just because it is so clearly a working library (as we academics are bound to notice): the books are in several languages, are put together by subject, and include pamphlets and other oddities—where so many stately home libraries seem to have bought their books by the yard and never opened them. The cabinet, too, shows the delightful quirkiness of Scott's collecting. It has some relics in it, of course: a lock of Bonnie Prince Charlie's hair; a piece of Mary Queen of Scot's dress; a pocketbook used by Flora Macdonald. But it also has a piece of oatcake found on a dead Highlander at the battle of Culloden, the final fight of the Jacobite rebellion (which someone must have been delighted to sell to Scott). There is also a box made of wood from the mulberry tree planted by Shakespeare, a lock of Nelson's hair, Rob Roy's skene-dhu, and now a lock of Scott's own hair.

If pilgrimages are made to writers' houses to feel the presence of the writer, to touch the real, Scott's house is full of such mementos of the real, such markers of his own obsession with uncovering the past, his own antiquarian love of the object touched by history: not just any oatcake but a morsel from the battlefield that sealed the fate of the Scots. No one but Scott would have put together this collection (and the few additions are in exactly the same vein: the lock of his own hair is labeled with how it was cut and who preserved it and who presented it—each thing needs its narrative). There are some great art collections, like the Frick in New York, where the owner's personality is vividly on show. Abbotsford really does capture something about Scott, not just in the baronial pile as dreamhouse, but in the idiosyncrasy of the collected objects. I could see why Victorian visitors published lists of Scott's things, and why the host as speaking guide to the collection is such a frequent figure in Scott's writing and in writing about Scott. In Abbotsford, it was easy to imagine Scott explaining, "And this piece of oatcake . . ."

Two other quirky items caught my attention. The armory is a long thin corridor of a room, with gargoyles at the ends of its ribbed ceiling beams and racks of muskets and crossed swords all across the walls. But it does have a pair of cartoonish drawings, one of which, the label solemnly announces, is certainly based on historic truth. It shows a woman lifting a silver cover from a dish at a banquet table to reveal a set of spurs. One of Scott's ancestors relied on rustling from English flocks for his family's food. When the stock of his stolen animals was running low, his wife would serve up spurs at the table to remind him it was time to go a-thieving again or leave the family hungry. "History painting" is the grandest of academy genres. Here we get a nicely defla-tionary account of local, family history—epic tinged with the parodic, the family hero as cattle stealer. "Certainly based on truth" is the sort of ironic label Scott would have loved to add.

In the drawing room, the most obviously grand public space in the house, we see the poshest side of Scott. The wallpaper is green, deco-rated Chinese painted paper. There are gas fittings—this was one of the first houses to be lit by gas, which the estate itself produced. There is an elegant Portuguese ebony escritoire, which cost the huge sum of one hundred guineas. Over the fireplace is a massive picture of Scott and his dog by the society portraitist Sir Henry Raeburn. The drawing room, the room for public performance, provides a suitably grandiose set for (self-)display. And in one cabinet, there stands a large silver urn, presented to Scott by Byron, containing the remains of ancient Greeks, dug up in Athens—"Attic bones," as the inscription on the urn puts it. Scott and Byron exchanged gifts like Homeric heroes (the description is Scott's), literary lion to literary lion, and with explicit recognition of their shared, gentlemanly love of things classical. The urn reveals

Scott at the center of a set of a literary network, surrounded in his house by gifts that delineate that network. (Wordsworth and Brontë, two famous solitaries, and the subjects of the next two chapters, both came here, Brontë only after Scott's death.) As in Homer, the objects that surround the heroes come with a history of their giving. Unlike so many country houses, here you can see how Scott's physical world was put together as a map of his social relations.

Artists struggled to capture this intellectual network of Scott, just as biographers struggled to capture his power over the imaginations of his readers. There are pictures on the walls at Abbotsford that represent the fifteen-year-old Scott meeting Robert Burns, his immediate ancestor as great Scottish poet, and others that represent him in a room with all the luminaries of the age (a similar picture is in Rydal Mount, Wordsworth's house). It doesn't seem to matter that there was no occasion on which the gang actually was all together like this. What seems to have been important is to try and express what Scott means: the center of an intellectual world, the hub of writing. Every bit of Abbotsford goes toward the construction of this image of Scott.

We ended, as if we had dined splendidly, on the terrace, and then strolled down to the tree-lined river—and the classic view back up to the house, the view that is meant to capture the vision, steadily and whole. Abbotsford had turned out to be a real surprise to start our pilgrimage. It gets some twenty-six thousand visitors a year, but on the sunny summer's day we visited there were barely a dozen. (I was told they got more when it rained . . .) The gardens were in full bloom; the river chortled away; I could sit and read Scott by the old game larder on the terrace, and wander down to the Tweed through the buttercups and forget-me-nots with my friends and my loving wife, happy, arm in arm, like the hero and heroine at the end of a Scott novel. That all helps. . . . But what really surprised me was that the house reeked of Scott—not so much Scott the novelist or poet, but Scott the manipulator of his image, Scott the keen antiquarian, Scott the networker, Scott the dream builder. Scott was, in the old phrase, the presiding genius of the place—the motivating creative force behind the pomposities and curiosities of the material world of Abbotsford. Precisely because it was such a self-consciously constructed environment, the vision of one man, and barely added to, the self kept peeping through where it might be least expected: in a display cabinet, in a cartoon, in the profusion of things, things labeled, with stories attached.

The Scott who appeared at Abbotsford was the inventor of tradition, finding history in things, "the lord of the buried past." With the cabinet of bizarrely interconnected knickknacks in the library of well-thumbed books, you might just imagine Scott the antiquarian tour guide of local and national history holding forth, with wry passion, about his writer's things, his collection. I am not sure this was the Scott that drew Victorian visitors to make the laborious pilgrimage to Abbotsford, but it sounds a lot like the Scott that Washington Irving delighted in meeting. In the eccentric vividness of Scott's own love of material things as relics of a story of the past, I could see an inkling of why writers' houses might fire the imagination. I don't think I learned a great deal about Scott's books or Scott's writing—and visitors to Abbotsford when he was alive said they were never aware of him as a writer, as he did his work secluded in his study, before most his guests came down for breakfast. Scott's presence was palpable, not, for me, in the mark of his buttocks on the chair in his study or in the folded trousers in the display case in the hall, but in the personality expressed by his things, as he put them together, in the museum of himself as a public figure.

3

PANTING UP THE ENDLESS ALP OF LIFE

IT WAS A REAL shock to me, when I was lying in bed with my wife, chatting about pilgrimage in a desultory way, and she sleepily confessed that she couldn't recall ever reading any poem of Wordsworth. Now, when you grow up in different cultures—London and New York, in our cases—lots of crucial childhood references are bound to be different. I had never seen *Mr. Ed*, with its talking horse, or *Mister Rogers' Neighborhood* (though I have heard the excruciating lyrics of its theme song, "It's a beautiful day in the neighborhood," innumerable times in excruciating and malicious wifely falsetto), and she has never seen *Magic Roundabout* and consequently never understood why, when she said to the children "Time for bed," I would winningly add, "said Zebedee." But this was something different. This was *Wordsworth*.

I actually snuck down next morning—feeling like I was going through pockets for incriminating credit card receipts—and dug out my wife's battered *Norton Anthology*, carried, like my Scott, unread from house to house, throughout our marriage. After all, my wife has four degrees, a liberal arts education, and, despite not always taking it kindly when I interrupt her work with suggested reading lists of Victorian novels, she gets through more literature than most, and much more than most lawyers. But it looked like she hadn't been winding me up. It was true. There were pages of Shelley and Coleridge and Wallace Stevens with pencil annotations from lectures and classes. But the Wordsworth pages were as untrammeled as Lake District snow. Somehow Wordsworth had been skipped.

My shock wasn't just because I had imagined that every child could recite at least "I wandered lonely as a cloud" from schooldays, even if, like me, they had no idea why a cloud would be lonely: surely we all immediately think of Wordsworth when we see a host of golden daffodils growing in a park, even Central Park? Rather, for me, this baffling and unexpected absence of Wordsworth in the mind wasn't (just) an issue of some supposed ideal of cultural literacy, but something far more personal, especially from my soul's partner.

When I was a plump and inwardly inclined teenager, with a passion for literature (among other, less salubrious fantasies), two parts of my life collided to make Wordsworth a figure in my imagination to rival Joni Mitchell and Tottenham Hotspur Football Club. First, I spent a huge amount of time climbing mountains, camping, and expeditioning with friends. Part of my adolescent reaction to the urban and highly materialistic culture of North London was to rough it in the hills. Iceland may mean ash clouds and banking crises to some: my first and cherished recollection is of wild terrain, sleeping on glaciers, struggling across torrents with my mates. Second, Wordsworth happened to be a set text for my final years at high school, my A levels. In those different educational days, from fifteen to eighteen years old I studied only Latin, Greek and English literature. This means that I still can't change a plug, but I did read swaths of Wordsworth's poetry and learned loads of it by heart. I studied plenty of literary criticism too, directed by our gay, jazz-playing Leavisite teacher, who took us back to his apartment to hear the vibes on Modern Jazz Quartet disks and gave us theater tickets for new experimental shows. I strived, like a Royal Shakespearean actor, to say "nature" with its full, rounded Wordsworthian power.

So, as I lay in bed, I remembered a particular morning in the Lake District in the north of England when I was seventeen years old. The previous day had been one of the most frightening hikes of the whole camping group's life, caught at high altitude in complete white-out, when the conditions became so fierce that the snow, sky and ground seemed an unbroken, hostile whiteness. Loss of bearings, freezing temperatures, and desperate strain just to make out a shape from the blankness—it was terrifying and exhausting and very dangerous. The next day, I came out somewhat tousled from the hostel near Lake Windermere and the weather was astonishingly calm, and clear and sunny. The mountains all around were snow-covered, the water flat and reflective, the air sharply fresh and clean. I sat and stared and stared, overwhelmed by the beauty, uncannily peaceful. And like a soundtrack Wordsworth began to play in my mind—those extraordinary lines from "Tintern Abbey" when he talks about his feelings for the natural world, and the impact of looking at—being in—nature. He recalls "that blessed mood" when we feel "the motion of our human blood almost suspended":

> While with an eye made quiet by the power
> Of harmony, and the deep power of joy,
> We see into the life of things.

This is what he meant, I said to myself, transfixed, on the lakeside. Now, seventeen is a good age to be a bit pretentious (it has taken me years to realize that I didn't actually understand all the lyrics of the Joni Mitchell songs I hummed while hiking). But that period of my life still seems formative to me, when I was discovering what I really cared about, while trudging the hills in earnest conversation with my friends, and when, at the same time, I was suspecting that literature was going to be my life and livelihood (or so I hoped). It felt suddenly rather hollow that my wife had someone else, where my Wordsworth sat: that we hadn't shared Wordsworth. I wanted to get up immediately and read her "Tintern Abbey," there and then. But despite a pretentious adolescence, I am not yet in a relationship where we read poetry to each other in bed, much. And anyway it was late, and she had a case in court in the morning.

Oddly enough, my North London teenage response to Wordsworth now seems positively Victorian to me. As poetry through the nineteenth century became invested with the power to mold and change a life, so Wordsworth became the high priest of this new religious fervor. There were thousands of young men and women, who, like I did, found in Wordsworth a personal guide for their internal lives. But unlike Scott's or Byron's instant celebrity, Wordsworth's poetry was a slow-burner. Every student is meant to know that Wordsworth's earlier publications are seminal for the history of Romanticism and English literature, but like so many revolutionary works, they did not sell well at the start (though not as badly as the Brontës' now highly coveted first book of poetry, which sold precisely two copies). Scott sold thousands and thousands more volumes of *Marmion* than Wordsworth and Coleridge managed with their *Lyrical Ballads*, at least in its first years. But Wordsworth's poetry came to take up a quite remarkable place for the Victorians, some decades after it was published. Wordsworth became a famous radical when he was already in slowing middle age—and from that time on he had an unparalleled status and influence.

The easiest way to see how much Wordsworth affected his readers is from a quotations like this one, from a fan letter written to him in 1841, when the poet was already seventy-one years old:

> Instruction in all, which it chiefly behoves to know—humbler reliance in the Divine rule—fuller love of Man—deeper & holier sympathies with Nature—in success, self-diffidence—in trial & suffering the stay and comfort of religious wisdom—are lessons which I, in common with thousands—owe to those works [of yours].

This breathless, hyperbolic praise was sent to the poet by the sober Sir John Simon, surgeon, medical professor, and the first chief medical officer of England. He wasn't alone. The young Charles Darwin enthusiastically read and reread *The Excursion*, another massive epic of journeying into the self (along with Lockhart's *Life of Scott*, with the third volume read out loud). Even the philosopher John Stuart Mill, depressed, austere, hyperintellectual, found in Wordsworth's poems "a medicine for my state of mind . . . they expressed, not outward beauty but states of feeling, and of thought coloured by feeling, under the excitement of beauty": poetry rather than philosophy saved the philosopher's soul.

No surprise in the face of such intense responses, then, and with an eye on poetry as the new religion, that Wordsworth is (eventually) compared to the Bible. James Russell Lowell, poet, campaigner, critic from Harvard, sets the tone: "Wordsworth's better utterances have the bare sincerity, the absolute abstraction from time and place, the immunity from decay, that belongs to the grand simplicities of the Bible." Charles Kingsley, parson and author, celebrated him as "preacher and prophet of God's new and divine philosophy—a man raised up as a light in a dark time" (which is exactly what Kingsley himself would have liked to be, of course). For the American ornithologist Henry Hudson, even more extravagantly, Wordsworth was "the most spiritual and spiritualizing of all the English poets. . . . No poetry outside the Bible . . . can stand comparison with him in this respect."

We could easily extend this roll call of scientists, philosophers, politicians, writers. Across the board Victorians found in Wordsworth an anatomist of their internal life, a guide to morals and to feelings, a melancholic and inspirational explorer of memory, of friendship, and, above all, of man's place in nature, at a time when industrialization was changing the experience of modern living. He had his critics, of course, especially of his idealized picture of the child in nature, but no poet today has anything like this power and reach. In fact, it is hard to point to anything at all in our contemporary culture that could link such a range of professions and ideals with such heartfelt commitment (Joni Mitchell? football?). The glue of modern society seems altogether less intellectually and spiritually bracing. My brief moment by Lake Windermere, when Wordsworth seemed to have prepared and then flooded through my city boy's feelings, would probably seem for nineteenth-century readers rather conventional and low-key. Going to Wordsworth's house is the one leg of our pilgrimage where I might expect to get why people seem to love visiting writers' homes.

It helped my adolescent sensibility that Wordsworth was a young radical who went to France to share in the French Revolution. He had a child there with a French girl, a fact—cool enough for a wishful 1970s schoolboy, insensitive to her misery—that was studiously kept from his official biography for decades, though he continued to visit his former lover discreetly, even after his own marriage. He was friends with radical thinkers and poets, and wrote self-consciously revolutionary poetry, promising the heightened language of ordinary men, in rejection of the arid classicism of a previous generation. But he retired in a staid middle age to the Lake District, with his wife and sister, and his poetry, at least his new poetry, seemed to lack the vision and the gleam of earlier years. Yet his greatest work, significantly called *The Prelude*, was published only after his death in 1850. He had worked on it since his twenties—he died aged eighty—and this fourteen-book epic is an engrossing account of his younger, revolutionary days and how his moral and intellectual life were formed by his encounters with nature. (Literary critics argue furiously and fruitlessly whether the first, unpublished version, from 1805 [thirteen books], or the 1850 version [fourteen books] is the one to read . . .) Tourists, many of them grand intellectual figures in their own right, came to visit Wordsworth as an old man, and he showed them his haunts and pointed out the sights, as they looked on him, a monument of his own literary self-depiction. His poetic credo cherished "the spontaneous overflow of powerful feelings" that stemmed from "emotion recollected in tranquillity," and in some ways, across the span of Wordsworth's poetic career, he was a tour guide to his own past.

It is strange, though, that just as Wordsworth returns obsessively to his youth, so writing about Wordsworth sent me straight back to my adolescent yearnings. This is part of how Wordsworth gets under your skin, I think. So much of his great poetry is about travel, a walk, a journey. "Tintern Abbey" dissects his feelings on making a trip back to the Wye Valley. *The Prelude* follows his life's journey—his pilgrimage, as he calls it—as he goes from the Lakes to Cambridge, to Paris, to London, and back to the Lakes: "A traveller I am And all my tale is of myself." The story of *The Excursion* is—yes—an excursion, where one of the chief, and rather clunkily symbolic, characters is called the Wanderer. Although on some of these poetic trips Wordsworth occasionally meets and talks to strangers, and although at points throughout *The Prelude* he does address a dear Friend, never actually named as Coleridge, Wordsworth likes to walk alone. Hazlitt puts the principle in a charmingly direct way: "I like to go by myself," he declares. "Nature is enough for me." Then, with sly provocation, he adds, "I cannot see the wit of walking and talking at the same time," for "An Englishman ought to do only one thing at a time" (that's a quotation, neatly reused, from the practical political reformer William Cobbett). What's Hazlitt's aim in solitary, silent walking? "From the point of yonder rolling cloud I plunge into my past being . . ." Well, so too with Wordsworth. As he walks, and responds to the wonders of nature around him, his best conversations are between who he is today and his old self. His walking is always interrupted, as some scene or moment captivates him. (Do you have to be still to be moved? The poet thinks as he walks, and measures out his metrical rhythm by feet, but it is the moment of arrest when the most powerful feelings flow.) As his journey of life hesitates and turns back on itself, he views his self in process: "Many wanderings have left behind, Remembrances not lifeless." Wordsworth roams through his memories and desires, tracing the anatomy of his inner being—a walking cure, as Freud might have put it.

The dramatic scene of Wordsworth's poetry is again and again a man thrown back into his memories, reflecting on past and present feelings and the dynamics between who he was and who he is and who—young and old—he wants to be, politically, socially, intellectually. Even a poem as soppy as "Daffodils" is tinged with this reflective inwardness: "For oft when on my couch I lie, In vacant or in pensive mood, They flash upon that inward eye, Which is the bliss of solitude." The whole point of seeing those fluttering and dancing flowers is to remember them years later, in the bliss of solitude, and draw some emotional strength from the memory. Wordsworth encourages all his readers to wander and wonder, and to look back at where you have come from. The Victorians knew that they were obsessed with biography and autobiography, the "devotional literature of individualism." They saw this passion as one of the telling symptoms of their specifically modern culture, and in Wordsworth they found the poet laureate of self-analysis.

So what a cliché I was to think about my youthful rambles in the beauty and danger of the Lake District, and in the literature of my adolescent years, as I lay in bed—on my couch—reflecting on what it would be like not to know Wordsworth. When, after dinner one night a little later, I did decide to read "Tintern Abbey" to my wife, over-emotionally, it was a slightly too Victorian scene.

Now, Scott's Abbotsford was visited by its guests for Scott's sake, and many of the guests were famous names. Without Scott's fiction and a powerful imagination, as Washington Irving found, the landscape in the neighborhood was rather dull and unimpressive. But the Lake District was a pull before Wordsworth, and, then as now, it wasn't just poetry and self-analysis that led people onto pleasure boats or up mountain tracks. But with Wordsworth, the Lakes took on a new role in literary tourism. Wordsworth, of course, had his friends and visitors too—Coleridge chief among them—but, in a way quite different from Abbotsford, the Lakes and Wordsworth's houses themselves after his death became places to inhabit, to commune with literary heritage. Thomas Arnold, the historian and pioneering headmaster of Rugby School, made famous for us by *Tom Brown's Schooldays*, bought Fox How, a house in the same valley as Wordsworth's Rydal Mount. His son, Matthew Arnold, who became an arbiter of Victorian cultural taste, a poet and famous lecturer and essayist, duly romped around the hills in a Wordsworthian idyll. Charlotte Brontë, among many others, came and stayed with the Arnolds. Beatrix Potter, trailing *Peter Rabbit*, came to live here (and for reasons I do not quite fathom, thousands of Japanese now come to see her farm in particular). Arthur Ransome plotted *Swallows and Amazons* around the Lakes and hills, in those happy days before health and safety regulations.

Mrs. Humphry Ward, the best-selling late Victorian novelist, whom Virginia Woolf and her trendy pals scornfully giggled about for being fat and out of date, was Matthew Arnold's niece and Thomas Arnold's granddaughter: she was proudly an Arnold. She knew the countryside around Grasmere as "the valley of Wordsworth and Arnold; the valley where Arnold's poet-son rambled as a boy; where, for me, the shy and passionate ghost of Charlotte Brontë still haunts the open doorway of Fox How; where poetry and generous life and ranging thought still have their home": a landscape full of the glories of the literary past. She even remembered—she claimed—meeting the old Mrs. Wordsworth at Rydal Mount (William died the year before she was born): "I can still recall the childish feeling that this was no common visit and the house no common house—that a presence still haunted it. Instinctively, the childish mind said to itself 'Remember!'—and I have always remembered." I don't want to be cynical, but she would say that, wouldn't she, granted how anxious she was about her literary genealogy and heritage; she had been only five years old at the time. Fifty-five years after she felt a presence haunting Rydal Mount, she rented the house to live in. On one of the first nights there, her daughter Dorothy had a hair-raising vision. She saw "an old man, sitting in an arm chair by the window," she reported, "looking straight in front of him with a rapt expression." This was exactly the spot where the elderly Wordsworth had watched over his sister Dorothy's final sickbed. Mrs. Humphry Ward was so enthralled by her daughter's experience that she contacted the Psychical Society. There is a long history of literary ghosts at Rydal—of feeling the presence of the author.

Even Dove Cottage has its literary ghosts. Thomas de Quincey, best known for his autobiographical masterpiece *Confessions of an Opium Eater*, rented it after Wordsworth moved out. He was one of the first and most passionate of Wordsworth fans, all too keen to live in the master's aura. And there he had one of his most frightening visitations. One day, a knock was heard at the door, and there stood a turbaned Malay. De Quincey's maidservant had never before seen Asiatic dress and desperately called the master, who was transfixed by the scene of his homely English girl standing in awe at the "sallow and bilious skin of the Malay, enamelled or veneered with mahogany, by marine air, his small, fierce restless eyes, thin lips, slavish gesture and adoration." De Quincey did not know what to do, so—of course—he spoke some lines of Homer to him, on the grounds that Greek was the most Eastern language he knew. The conversation was not a success. The man was begging, it seemed, so de Quincey offered him a large piece of opium, "enough to kill three dragoons and their horses." The guest, shockingly, ate the lump in one gulp and walked off. For months de Quincey had terrible dreams of the Malay lying dead somewhere on the roads, so far from home. This reads like a nightmarish parody of a Wordsworth encounter with a beggar: no profound wisdom exchanged, no touching insight into character, no recognition of man's place in nature; rather, alienation, false gifts, fear, and worry. Wandering in the Lakes does not always lead to the Wordsworthian experience. There were other pilgrims on these roads too.

I boarded the train again in Edinburgh to go south into the Lake District. To take a train to Wordsworth's home is to traverse a cusp in history. George Stephenson, who invented the Rocket, the first locomotive engine to be touched with celebrity status, opened the Liverpool and Manchester Railway in 1830, the year of Scott's death. (A Member of Parliament was killed by the train at the opening ceremony, but the show went on . . .) By the time Charlotte Brontë went to Brussels in 1842, the train from Leeds to London was familiar enough an experience to moan about it being late. By 1850 the network traversed the whole country.

The train network changed the landscape of Britain, as it did for America, both physically and conceptually. The railway tracks and smoky engines cut swaths through the countryside. In America it opened new territory. In Britain, people, magazines, books, materials could be rushed around the country at an unheard-of rate, as what were once products for a market became commodities in the Market. This was industrialization, progress, modernity—feared and lauded in equal measure. Time itself seemed to speed up. Distances shrank. Trains annihilated old understandings of space and time, and a traveler's relation to the world. From the train at speed, the foreground was no longer visible, and, as Ruskin lamented, "all that you can know, at best, of the country you pass is its geological structure and its general clothing": "travelling becomes dull in exact proportion to its rapidity." For Wordsworth and the Lake District, the result was an influx of tourists. Wordsworth himself publicly opposed the extension of the railway to Low How, at the head of Lake Windermere: "The staple of the district is, in fact, its beauty, and its character of seclusion and retirement," he wrote. Perhaps he thought trains destroyed the countryside's peace; perhaps, for all his meaningful encounters with vagrants on the bridleways, he didn't want the massed workers from Manchester actually turning up in his valley. But here we were, not quite as smug and self-serving as politicians banging on about their environmental credentials, but well aware that by resisting the car and the plane we were doing the right thing. For Mrs. Gaskell's Cranford the train was the snorting, noisy, dirty sign of the brash arrival of modern machine culture; for us moderns, it has become the clean, green option.

The train into Windermere is a slow little two-carriage fellow, full of climbers and cyclists. When the train services were starting in the nineteenth century and for many years afterward, English trains and American trains looked quite different and prompted quite different social experiences. English carriages had compartments with a row of four or six seats facing another row of seats. In some trains it was impossible to move between compartments; others had a corridor on the outside. There's many a film whose plot turns on the configuration of compartments and corridors. American trains usually had single long carriages with multiple seats (as most English trains now have too). The clichés of the bandit train holdup wouldn't really work if the bandits had to go compartment to compartment. The difference stems from a different idea of a railway. When the English train system was established, trains followed well-established coach routes, and the trains were designed like a string of stagecoaches on tracks—the inside of each compartment was like the inside of a stagecoach, enclosed, passengers facing each other. American railways, by contrast, were usually opening new territory, and they took as their model the riverboat, which had been the standard transport through the broad, as yet unbuilt-up areas of the American interior. Hence, the long, open carriages. The English found themselves in a private space with strangers: hence the journey in awkward silence, or carefully scripted banalities. The American trains had a more convivial, party feel. Dickens, for all his love of characters and encounters, was horrified by the intimacy of American travel. Americans, in turn, were baffled by the starched formality of the British at close quarters. For American and British Victorian travelers, making their pilgrimages to writers' houses, culture clash began the moment they stepped onto the train.

For reasons too mundane and complicated to explain (a case blowing up in court, a family scene, a few urgent e-mails, a gap in a diary . . .), for this leg of my journey, I was now traveling with Daniel, another lawyer, once a lecturer in English literature, and an old friend from the same high school, though, two years below me, he didn't, it seems, do Wordsworth at A level. We had our bikes, and pottered out of the station at Windermere for the nine-mile ride to Grasmere. As a don in Cambridge, I cycle every day to work, around the university, to the library and the market. Daniel doesn't cycle, I found out, as I waited impatiently at the top of every rise. His borrowed bike lost its chain; the seat hurt; his backpack was uncomfortable. (I discovered the next morning that he had brought a snorkel and mask with him for the pool at the hotel—which is only one version of traveling light). But even with the relentless traffic, the ride is lovely: round Windermere to the north, close along the placid, dark Rydal Water, and down to Grasmere, with views across the lakes to the hills around. It's rich country now, with big houses and hotels and expensive boats in the marina. But fifteen minutes from the road you can climb into magnificent solitude in the hills.

Dove Cottage is set back a few yards from the road, shielded by

Dove Cottage: Wordsworth's home, tucked back from the
road and set into the hillside.

trees, a low dry-stone wall, and some later Victorian houses. It is an
attractive whitewashed cottage, architecturally undistinguished but
pleasingly pastoral on a sunny day in the summer. The only way to see
the house is with a tour given by one of the interns, ten young people
who spend a year each on a traineeship in museum studies at Dove Cottage. A dozen of us, a motley crew of visitors, crammed into the first
room, the dining room, for the well-rehearsed spiel. The room is small,
with a single wood beam and a single mullioned window, with a small
window seat beneath it. The ceiling is low, the floor hard flagstones.
It is dark, even in summer. The bare furniture is Wordsworth's or the
family's, and the one picture is a horrid sub-sub-Landseer portrait of a
dog, a Dandie Dinmont called Pepper given to Wordsworth's children
by Sir Walter Scott. The house had been a pub, and Wordsworth was
probably its first private tenant. The front door opens straight into the
dining room (which would have been one of the drinking rooms). No

expansive hallway with two grand staircases here. Coming from Abbotsford, the contrast was comprehensive.

Dorothy's bedroom and the kitchen are similar in their simplicity and poverty. The walls of the children's small bedroom—the Wordsworths had their three children in this cottage too—are papered with newspapers. I wondered if the children read the words as they tried to fall asleep, or took their surroundings for granted, with barely a glance at the headlines. (The country music star Loretta Lynn also has newspaper for wallpaper in the replica of her childhood bedroom, in her rags-to-riches autobiographical theme park in Kentucky.) The cottage still has a vivid hand-to-mouth feel: the kids' walls were papered with what there was. The larder is a small back room built into the side of the hill to keep temperatures cool even in the hot months; the coalhole opens straight into the kitchen, but the coal, delivered by the wonderfully named Mr. Ashburner, had to be carried through the dining room; there is a coffee grinder on the workspace, but no running water in the house. The guide—more interested, as my Friend noted, in personal hygiene than political philosophy—duly recounted that the Wordworths washed themselves only once every couple of weeks and their clothes once every four weeks, a process that took a whole day down in the village. He passed round a twig used as a toothbrush. We all stared at it and passed it on.

The same theme ran through the bedroom. There was a short double bed, a four-poster, actually brought over from Rydal: this design was useful, explained the guide, because with open ceilings, you need a canopy to protect you from the rats and mice above and, in the case of Dove Cottage, from the rain too, which came through the rafters. On the bed was Wordsworth's very small traveling case, with room just for his nightshirt and a bare change of clothes. "But as he didn't wash . . . ," continued the guide, reveling ghoulishly in the dirt of the past. Worsdworth's study upstairs, another low room with a single window, had no desk. He dictated; Dorothy, his sister, or Mary, his wife, took down the verses on a writing-board rested on her knees. So Wordsworth would walk the hills, composing as he went, tramping out his rhythms—he would quieten if he met a stranger, so as not to appear mad. (Nowadays it would no doubt be assumed he had a hands-free mobile phone.) Then he would return and recite the verse to the woman to write down. "And here you can see the couch," said the guide, with a disconcerting literalism, "on which he lay as described in 'Daffodils.'" The symbiotic life—intricately, emotionally interconnected—of the three adults in the close quarters of the tiny rooms was easy to dramatize in one's mind—and offered some sort of way toward understanding why Wordsworth didn't just write down his own poems. Those first years at Dove Cottage, poor, unwashed, and writing great poetry and engaging passionately in each other's daily lives, physical and mental, writing letters and journals and poetry about the process—these were paradigmatic years for the image of the Romantic artist.

Dove Cottage is offered to the visitor first as an example of daily life, and second as the scene of an extraordinary poetic exuberance. What is left out is the oddity of the move itself. Dove Cottage is in the middle of nowhere: Dorothy and William walked many miles across the hills to reach it the first time on a cold winter's day. The cottage was damp; the fire upstairs smoked so badly it could not be used for a public room. Even nearby friends lived ten miles away. Wordsworth had been in France in the excitement of the Revolution; he had lived in the West Country while writing the *Lyrical Ballads* with Coleridge. He had a small legacy to live on. But now he chose to return north and to find an obscure and miserable place to make a home, as far as possible from the centers of literary and political life. And we were there on a perfect summer's day: in winter it would have been even more unremittingly shut off. Wordsworth has an intensely political as well as an intellectual and psychological strand to his poetry. His poetry stretches across not only the French Revolution but the growth of the British Empire (the backdrop to all these houses), and his passion for the natural world as a guide for the soul is contemporary with Marx's excoriating account of the industrial revolution and its destructive force on human relations. The move to Dove Cottage seems an act of self-immolation—yet from Dove Cottage emerged what Hazlitt called a "new view or aspect of nature" based on the revelation of "the heart of the retired and lonely student of nature." Wordsworth retired into himself, and turned his withdrawal into an act of poetic remembrance. Each day he would walk the huge expanses of the mountains and stare at the lakes and the trees and sky around, and then retreat into the small, dark rooms of Dove Cottage to recite. He called these his Golden Years.

There is a rather good, if somewhat solemn, museum now next to the house, which has recordings of poems recited by modern poets (you listen on headphones), some great manuscripts, including the *Prelude*—the Wordsworth Trust at Dove Cottage owns a vast percentage of all the Wordsworth autograph manuscripts—and such oddities as Wordsworth's skates (about which the Nobel Prize winner Seamus Heaney has written a short poem and recorded it for the museum, along with one about how Dorothy must have been really depressed or lonely or sad not to have noticed her coalman was called Mr. Ashburner). You can see the fair copies made by Mary and Dorothy, and Dorothy's journals; pictures of famous chaps and so forth. If you want a museum about a poet this is a pretty good example of what can be done. We wandered around with the somewhat lugubrious supermarket trudge that means you have been in the museum a bit too long, hoping already your companion will say, "Let's have a drink!" That's the advantage for me of going to museums with my wife: we know each other's attention span, and we both like the idea of cake. Even with a friend there are more sterling proprieties to observe . . .

We walked the mile to our restaurant that evening, a rather pious vegetarian country house hotel. There were three other couples there. Within three minutes we had discovered the couple next to us were Israeli, he a supreme court judge, she a lawyer; that their daughter and Daniel had coincidentally been at the same wedding in Jerusalem three days earlier; that they themselves had been in Cambridge on that day and had been at a party I would have attended had I not been traveling back myself from New York; and that he had been visiting the House of Lords as a guest of the English judiciary. We quickly established a political negotiating ground, a social framework, and continued with Jewish geography. ("How long have you known each other?" asked one of the other couples, eavesdropping, after the Israelis had left. "We just met," we explained, which clearly didn't quite satisfy them, used to the silence of railway compartments and the grim reticence of English social politeness.) Wordsworth had walked nearly a whole day to reach Dove Cottage, and spent months away from London, years absent from his child in France. Here we were, having reached Grasmere from New York, Jerusalem, and London in the last couple of days, discussing this week's politics in the Senate and the Knesset and Parliament. I guess one can idealize slow travel, the pilgrimage of the poetic soul, but still get a thrill out of the prospect of slipping over to New York for the weekend.

Next morning, I woke, completely alert, at sunrise. Instead of turning over and going back to sleep, I dressed and left the hotel in silence and climbed up behind into the hills above Grasmere. There was no noise but the birds and the occasional sheep bleating, parentally. Within half an hour I was on the top of Silver How and could see five lakes below—Windermere, Rydal, Grasmere, and the two little ones to the west of Windermere. The weather was bitingly clear. There were trees sharply and unmovingly reflected in the water of Rydal, hundreds of feet below me. I could see the blunt monster of Scafell, tallest mountain in England, to the summit. As I dipped over the coll into the bowl between the peaks around Silver How, the air became quite still; dozens of moths, no bigger than a thumbnail, flittered around the little tarns, the black water studded with deep green lily pads. A single bird rushed past. The ground, even in summer, was what Wordsworth calls the "plashy earth," with coarse long grass and brown dampness oozing between every stalk. The lack of any car noise, any sound of humans, was stilling. I stood motionless for minutes and gazed, and it felt like a decision—a decision to move back down to the world of getting and spending—even to start to walk again. There was the pool, the sauna, and breakfast, with smoked fish and poached eggs, back at

WORDSWORTH'S HOUSE, RYDAL MOUNT.

Rydal Mount: drawn for a tour guide in 1897, Wordsworth's grand house is depicted in the style of stately home to suit his new status as grand poet.

the hotel. But it felt as though I had saved up a touch of Wordsworth's idea of repose for the months to come, when the world is too much with us.

It is good to visit Rydal Mount after Dove Cottage. Rydal, three miles down the road toward Windermere, lying further back from the road on a low hill, is set within spectacular, multilevel terraced gardens, cut into the hillside, and beneath a mountain that frames the view of the house from the lawns. The grounds and the upstairs rooms look out across the shimmers of Rydal Water through the trees. Rydal Mount is a large, well-proportioned, and attractive Victorian house. The dining room has three windows, two beams across the ceiling, which is painted white, a full-size dining table with carved chairs (the table at Dove Cottage was a folding one, and folded away in the kitchen just to allow visitors into the restricted space of the dining room there). It is a room for entertaining, and for meals with more than one course. (Dorothy described their diet in the early days at Dove Cottage as milk for breakfast and potatoes in the evening.) The hallway has wooden floors, with a grand staircase, with square turns, lit by a skylight in the roof above. From the hall you can step into the drawing room and library, which were knocked through into one splendid room in 1968. The ceilings are high. There are large windows overlooking the garden and bookcases with a selection of reading matter (nothing like Scott's—this is a family house with some standard classics on the shelves). The house is still lived in: there are modern books and pictures too, as well as innumerable paintings of the Wordsworths. There is a license prominently displayed: you can get married or have a civil partnership here, and have a nice party where Wordsworth sat and Mrs. Humphrey Ward's daughter saw his ghost.

The portraits that cover the walls provide some sense of the continuous history of the house. The Wilkins portrait (1831) captures a fine idea of the craggy inwardness of the poet, but perhaps the most striking image is the full-scale portrait of the elderly Wordsworth by William Inman, which hangs over the fireplace (1844). Inman was an American artist who had been commissioned by the University of Pennsylvania to make a portrait of Wordsworth for the university (the letters of thanks are on display in a cabinet at Rydal Mount). Inman, with his young daughter, came across from America and stayed two months with the Wordsworths. Dorothy so liked the picture, she commissioned this copy. It is a mark of the new iconic status of Wordsworth that a university in America wanted to decorate its halls with an image of him. Wordsworth had become the inspirational figurehead of literature, so important that, even with the anti-British sentiment that we often find in American artistic culture at this period, he transcended such nationalism. On the wall here is his first refusal of the post of poet laureate, a position he accepted only after he had been assured that it came with no duties or obligations. Rydal Mount is the home of a grand figure of literature.

The bedrooms upstairs are light and airy, with beautiful views across the gardens toward the lake, especially Dorothy's, the corner room; the light filtered through the trees and shrubs is green and mellow. Wordsworth's daughter Dora accompanied him on his trips until she married (at age thirty-seven, against her father's initial wishes). She returned to Rydal Mount to be nursed by her mother in her final illness, and when she died, aged only forty-three, from the consumption she had had since her youth, Wordsworth was broken with grief. Her bedroom is still Dora's room, and the field at the bottom of the garden toward the church is planted out with daffodils in her memory (the gate on the memorial field has a sign that, here of all places, acts as a poetic *memento mori*: "One Way: No Return"). There are genealogical charts of the Wordsworth family across the walls in Wordsworth's attic study on the third floor, and pictures of the more recent generations in the library. Where a museum tries to fix a moment of time and holds the gem up to the gaze of the spectator, this is very much a family home, marked too by loss and the passing of time.

The move from Dove Cottage to Rydal Mount signals a wholesale change in the life of Wordsworth and his family. From the little dark rooms with newspaper on the walls, and the memories of long cold nights of intensity and solitude, Wordsworth becomes a man of standing, famous, a monument to his own early life, someone to be seen to visit. His first year at Rydal Mount is when the first edition of his collected works is published, and he becomes thus a sort of institution in the public eye. He continues to tinker with *The Prelude* in private, hugging it to himself, while publishing poems like the *Ecclesiastical Sonnets*, which even Wordsworth aficionados struggle to love. If there was something of a holy anchorite about his time at Dove Cottage, his "hermitage," as he calls it, at Rydal Mount he has become the saint in waiting, the sage to be consulted.

For the first time, his house had a real view. The Romantic movement made the idea of the picturesque fashionable. William Gilpin and other theorists in the eighteenth century had created a new way of seeing beauty in nature, and the craze for journeying to viewpoints to emote on the framed splendor of the natural world was so pervasive that it becomes a staple joke in Jane Austen. Catherine Morland in *Northanger Abbey* is given "a lecture on the picturesque" by Henry Tilney: "He talked of foregrounds, distances and second distances—side-screens and perspectives—lights and shades—and Catherine was so hopeful a scholar, that when they gained the top of Beechen Cliff, she voluntarily rejected the whole city of Bath, as unworthy to make part of a landscape." Despite Jane Austen's gentle satire, the Romantic garden is a *topos* of nineteenth-century understanding of geographical space and the place of the spectator within it. The Americans had William Cullen Byant's *Picturesque America*, a huge and expensive volume with nearly fifty engravings that nonetheless sold more than half a million copies in the 1870s, defining the landscape of America for a generation. Rydal Mount is a perfect example of the picturesque garden, with its carefully orchestrated perspectives of the lake, and then back to the house with the mountain behind, and the terraced gardens with its avenues and turns. Wordsworth at Rydal Mount became the master of this view of nature. Once he had been haunted by the cataract, and the mountains, "huge and mighty forms, that do not live Like living men, moved slowly through the mind By day, and were a trouble to my dream." Now he took tea on the terrace and talked of nature with his visitors. It's as if Dove Cottage is an element in a picturesque scene: the poor but pretty cottage framed by flowers. But Rydal Mount is a stage set for the poet as the spectator of all he surveys.

The gardens—this would have terrified poor de Quincey and his servant—had three or four Japanese visitors intently staring at each flowering bush and then strolling along the walks. The tour buses on the way to Beatrix Potter's farm often stop here, reversing slowly up the hill or making heavy rumbling turns in the small gravel car park. "They like gardens; they don't have much space at home for gardens," was the caretaker's offhand explanation (though I suppose the lure could be literature, shaming the parochial Brits with their ignorance of Japanese writers' houses; or it could just be a stop tours always make, with the tourists as baffled as we are as to why they are there). They certainly took no notice of two hairy Jews in bicycle helmets, talking of *The Prelude*. I wonder what Wordsworth, fresh from railing in the newspapers about how a train would disturb the seclusion of the Lake District, would make of the busloads of Japanese tourists arriving every day to spend forty minutes in his garden and, for those prebooked, to take tea and cake in the house itself. I am still not convinced I understand why writers' houses have the pull they do, but I am more than baffled by modern habits of holiday travel.

I have lived a long time now with Wordsworth's poetry in my head, and visiting Dove Cottage offered a bare but vivid screen on which to project a long-constructed image of the weird family life of husband, sister, and wife, and to wonder about the claustrophobia of the small dark rooms and the massy solitude of the mountains outside. But the transition between Dove Cottage and Rydal Mount seemed to embody an even more telling and melancholic narrative of Wordsworth's creative life. I had known for many years that Wordsworth had moved from Dove Cottage to Rydal Mount, but it was only when I saw the physical difference in the settings that I felt I could appreciate what the move really meant for Wordsworth's life as a public persona, his self-presentation, his sense of his own poetic journey. Has it changed my appreciation of Wordsworth? The image that will haunt me after this trip is the middle-aged Wordsworth, growing slowly older in the high comfort of Rydal Mount, holding on to *The Prelude*, a living, cherished, changing memorial and exploration of his earlier life and spirit. To let *The Prelude* go would have meant to fix something that Wordsworth could not bear to think final. It would mark an end—as, indeed, it did.

Dove Cottage on its own is a simple cottage, Rydal Mount an elegant villa. Neither tells you much about the poet as a poet or about the poet's personality, at least not in the way that Scott's museum of himself at Abbotsford does. But the houses together, together with the mountains around, help us tell a narrative of Wordsworth's creative life. Wordsworth himself spent most of his poetic work rehearsing his life's journey, so it is perhaps inevitable that as we journeyed we found ourselves talking about his poetry and his life, his life in poetry, his life as poetic narrative. I can't imagine that I will want to go back to Dove Cottage or Rydal Mount when I next come back to the Lake District to get my dose of mountain air and steep climbs. But I did notice that we both surreptitiously plucked a leaf from the garden in Rydal Mount to take home to London.

4

SEETHING IN YORKSHIRE

"HEATHCLIFF!, HEATHCLIFF!" I reckon I only have to write the name—it has to be twice, though—to get the Brontë myth up and running. Seething, dark, destructive passions across class and prudence, acted out against the seething, dark, destructive moors, and—this is where the myth really gets going—written by an intense, lonely young woman, roaming the hillside, struggling with her seething, dark, destructive passions and, inevitably, dying young, tragically. *Wuthering Heights* is often read for the first time during one's own seething period, and thanks also to the films—Laurence Olivier, seen by a staggering 220 million people by 1949, was Byronic and handsome enough to haunt many a dream—it has become the sort of cultural icon that means that you recognize the atmosphere even if you don't remember the plot.

Now, I cry at almost anything—poems, films, music—but I am not sentimental; I have spent most of my life working on Greek tragedy, where weeping is the result of the self-destructive, self-deceptive, violently ambitious hopes of humans. I am unconvinced by redemption, and hate the manipulative Hollywood climax of hugs and brave tears. For me, the nasty bleakness of *Wuthering Heights* tells it how it is. (I could never manage to talk fondly about *Anne of Green Gables*—another story of a young girl in rural hardship with literary aspirations, but with an ending of stomach-churning, redemptive relief—in the way my wife, the hardened lawyer, can reminisce about her childhood reading. Classicists learn early to mistrust the romantic . . .) But even so, I traveled with little expectation that the moors and Haworth could match Emily Brontë's vision of a harsh, traumatic landscape. It can be grim in Yorkshire, for sure, but I remembered reading W. G.

Sebald's disturbing book, *Rings of Saturn*, a walking tour of East Anglia, where the landscape emerges as a deserted, threatening, looming menace of buried anxieties. This vision depicted the same beaches and fields and woods where we went on holiday with our children: bustling villages, playful sands, old churches—thoroughly populated and quite giggly. I was happy enough to envisage East Anglia through Sebald's gloomy prose, and Yorkshire through Emily Brontë's, but I didn't expect the windows to crash, "Cathy" to be heard on the wind, or the rocks to be really menacing.

Wuthering Heights has had more than its fair share of influence on the Brontë myth. Charlotte and Anne actually both worked away from Haworth and the lure of the moors—Charlotte's time as a teacher in Brussels, when she fell in love with her boss and teacher, a married man, had a major impact on her imagination and her writing—but the sisters did all grow up at Haworth, with their reprobate brother, Branwell, and their gruff and demanding father, Patrick, they each wrote from Haworth, and returned home to Haworth for long periods of their short lives (while Emily never really left the moors). *Jane Eyre*, Charlotte's masterpiece, encourages a fixation on the Brontë house in a quite different way from any other of the other books and writers on this pilgrimage. It is a first-person narrative of a girl growing up: we look at the world through her eyes. Jane sits behind the curtain reading, she faces the violence and cruelty of a thoughtlessly vicious school, the social discomfort and even humiliations of life as a governess, the perils of love—and at every moment we follow the story through her feelings and worries and thoughts. The subtitle of the book is "An Autobiography," and *Jane Eyre* wrote the story of the self in a new and extraordinarily challenging way. The novel has its social criticism, for sure, which angered and provoked its first audience. But what really excited and confused its Victorian readers was that here, for once, was the internal life of a woman depicted in all its flaring intensity, insecurity, and complexity. It had, as George Lewes, George Eliot's partner, put it, a "strange power of subjective representation." Many books present the surface of Victorian life. With *Jane Eyre* we are led beyond the door, into the house, behind the curtain, and into the mind and heart of its heroine. Visiting Haworth isn't just a pilgrimage to gaze at the domestic space of a writer, but an invitation to a far more intimate exploration of a woman's mind.

Yet when *Jane Eyre* came out, there was no talk of Haworth or the moors. The novel was published under a pseudonym—Currer Bell—and when it became a sudden success, there was the usual fuss and bother about who the author really was (Thackeray, with hilarious misprision, first guessed it was A. W. Kinglake—an Old Etonian man-about-town who produced the standard history of the Crimean War!). But not everyone appreciated its anatomy of intimacy, its raw feelings about subjects that polite women did not discuss publicly at all. Matthew Arnold found in Jane nothing but "hunger, rebellion and rage." The *Quarterly Review* found the book politically subversive—and this is 1848, the year of revolutions: "We do not hesitate to say that the tone of mind and thought which has overthrown authority and violated every code, human and divine, abroad, and fostered Chartism and rebellion at home, is the same which has also written *Jane Eyre*." Charlotte Brontë, to her own surprise, was, above all, criticized for being "coarse." This did not stop the book from selling well, and men as well as women reported how they had read the book all night with tears in their eyes. It was actually another woman writer who set out to make Haworth central to the Brontë myth, and she did a brilliant job.

Mrs. Gaskell is best known today, I suppose, for the Cranford stories, much beloved of actresses of a certain age and the BBC commissioning editors. Her first novels were aggressively polemical political works about poverty and the brutalities of industrial culture (and full of mawkish death scenes). But Mrs. Gaskell had made friends with Charlotte Brontë and, after her friend had died, wrote and published her biography. This was one of the first biographies of a female author written by a woman, and it immediately established what we know as the myth of the Brontës. The biography caused a real stir. This was partly because the upper-class married woman accused of leading the young Branwell into debauchery—called, funnily enough, Mrs. Robinson, in anticipation of *The Graduate*—cried libel and demanded a rewrite. But its fame came mostly from its vivid and compelling picture of a poor family in a remote village discovering their own literary talent and cautiously bringing it before an amazed world. It focused on domestic, intimate matters, from underwear to reading books while baking, in a way that all the men's biographies of great men avoided. It was Mrs. Gaskell who made Haworth the key to the Brontë life, who painted the picture of the pure, thoroughly uncoarse sisters, loving the moors, tending their father and brother, producing great art in the humble Yorkshire home. After Mrs. Gaskell, Haworth became a site of pilgrimage.

Mrs. Gaskell's biography begins with a description of the parsonage. "Everything about the place tells of the most dainty order, the most exquisite cleanliness. The door-steps are spotless; the small old-fashioned window-panes glitter like looking-glass. Inside and outside of that house cleanliness goes up into its essence, purity." This is the inverse of the cleanliness of the Thornton drawing-room in *North and South*: here cleanliness is a sign of exquisiteness and, above all, of moral purity—a "dainty order" for a society that so feared coarseness and disorder. It is hard not to take spotlessness "inside and outside" as a metaphor. Charles Kingsley (whose *Water-Babies* shows an even more disturbing fixation with cleanliness) shows the effect of Mrs. Gaskell's spin starkly. Before the biography came out, he thought Charlotte Brontë rather disgusting; after the biography, he recognized her goodness and liked her books accordingly: "*Shirley* disgusted me at the opening: and I gave up on the writer and her books with the notion that she was a person who liked coarseness. How I misjudged her! . . . Well have you done your work, and given us the picture of a valiant woman made perfect by sufferings." Mrs. Gaskell blanked Charlotte's passion in Brussels, a scandalous truth that burst on the unwilling and fascinated Brontë fans only in 1913, and told the story of the sisters as an archetypal Victorian tale of endurance defeating disadvantage, coupled with a stoic suffering of the grimness of life, and plenty of mawkish death scenes. There were few signs of Charlotte's overwhelming internal misery, the "sense of weight, fear and desolation hard to express and harder to endure" that she recorded privately. She provided even fewer signs of jolliness or fun. Instead, the physical surroundings are made to take on all the oppressiveness of a tragic life. Mrs. Gaskell quotes from a friend's pilgrimage to Haworth:

> The country got wilder and wilder as we approached Haworth; for the last four miles we were ascending a huge moor, at the very top of which lies the dreary black-looking village of Haworth . . . a dreary, dreary place literally *paved* with rain-blackened tombstones. . . . There was an old man in the churchyard, brooding like a Ghoul over the graves, with a sort of grim hilarity on his face. I thought he looked hardly human; however, he was human enough to tell us the way.

You can almost hear the sigh of relief when the house itself turns out to be "scrupulously clean and neat," and, somewhat bathetically, everyone "began talking very comfortably." Mrs. Gaskell, more even than Emily Brontë herself, created the image of the house in the churchyard, the dark moors encroaching, the wind and rain as a pathetic fallacy of the girls' souls. That is what you are meant to see when you get to Haworth.

Mrs. Gaskell is equally directive about the hills around, as she imagines our approach. No dancing daffodils here. The view is "crowned with wild, bleak moors—grand, from the ideas of solitude and loneliness which they suggest, or oppressive from the feeling they give of being pent-up by some monotonous and illimitable barrier, according to the mood of mind in which the spectator might be." You are that spectator, and you are invited to feel loneliness, or oppressive monotony—but no Wordsworthian joy or mere sunniness: we are being prepared for the sisters' life as suffering artists.

In one bizarre way, the creation of the image has quite trumped the reality. Harriet Martineau, the celebrated Victorian feminist writer, wrote an obituary of Charlotte that dramatically depicted her looking out the window of the parsonage at the graves of her sisters in the graveyard just beneath it. Emily, as one might expect from Victorian bourgeois proprieties, was in fact buried in the crypt of the church, inside and quite concealed. Anne died and was buried many miles away, at Scarborough on the coast, a town she loved and had worked in. Charlotte duly joined Emily in the crypt. This inconvenient fact didn't stop Matthew Arnold from depicting Charlotte's grave too in an open graveyard, strewn with wind-blown grass—in a poem called "Haworth Churchyard," which recalls Harriet Martineau and Charlotte Brontë meeting in the Lake District at Fox How. Emily Dickinson later calls Charlotte's tomb, "all overgrown with cunning moss," as if it were untended on the moors. W. H. Charlton, a historian and vicar, in a poem that found its way into the frontispiece of a hagiographic Victorian book about Charlotte Brontë, prays that the graves of all three women be "wet with moorland showers." There are times when we all see what we need to see—and after Mrs. Gaskell's biography and Emily Brontë's longing for the wild heathland, it seemed obvious that the sisters were buried together, outside, in sight of the moors they loved, in the graveyard that defined the boundaries of their home life at Haworth. Except they weren't.

The parsonage at Haworth is a different beast from Scott's house at Abbotsford and Wordsworth's houses in the Lakes. Scott created Abbotsford self-consciously as an image of himself as author and his books as worldview. Wordsworth described his existence in Dove Cottage and Rydal Mount as an explorative image of a life in nature, and created a literary monument of his own life through his self-description in poetry. But Haworth Parsonage is a back-invention. The life of the sisters was told after their deaths by Mrs. Gaskell, and the myth has been spun out in multiple strands ever since. The parsonage has become a shrine full of myths: the children making up stories, as the first steps of literary genius; the sisters caring for father in the parlor, the icon of duty; the sisters staring out of the window, quietly passionate. The house has been turned by all those biographies of the Brontës, all those films, all those parodies, from a place to which the family moved

Haworth Parsonage in the 1870s: "One great change resulted from the publication of Mrs. Gaskell's work: Haworth and its parsonage became the shrine to which hundreds of literary pilgrims from all parts of the world began to find their way," Sir Thomas Wemyss Reid (1877).

because the father got a job there, to a foundation of literary genius and feminine soul. Virginia Woolf nicely captures how the house becomes integral to the self-expression of the artists: "Haworth and the Brontës are somehow inextricably mixed. It expresses the Brontës; the Brontës express it; they fit like a snail its shell." Like the snail, the sisters are organically housed in their shelter. But where Woolf is happy to dwell with the mystery (*"somehow* inextricably mixed"), I find it hard to shift my academic love of historical analysis. Her "somehow" was actually a story of cultural myth-making that started with Mrs. Gaskell.

Poor Anne never gets much of a look in, even with Mrs. Gaskell. But Emily, who was fiercely resistant to any form of public recognition, has had a remarkable journey in this myth-making. The erotic passions of *Wuthering Heights* and the sheer nastiness of Heathcliff in the second half of the book, which the famous Laurence Olivier film conveniently leaves out altogether, genuinely shocked Victorian readers, and for many it was simply impossible that a decent young, unmarried woman could have written such things. The book did get some great reviews as well as some stinkers, but Emily herself was repeatedly depicted as even coarser than Charlotte—a wild, bestial creature of the uncivilized moors. (It is strange to reflect that even Mrs. Gaskell stopped her own daughter from reading *Jane Eyre* until she was twenty years old.) Yet around the end of the century, Emily started to be depicted as spiritual, mystical, an untrammeled genius of nature. She even starts to overtake Charlotte as the sister who counts. Emily read German Romantic philosophy in German; she translated Virgil and took notes on the Greek tragedians, Aeschylus and Euripides; she read the literary periodicals and novels of the day. But she has now entered the modern imagination as a floaty, natural artist on the moors: from coarse, incomprehensibly passionate, to the epitome of mystical insight . . . a different myth, but one that seems keen to insist that the girl didn't actually read books and think.

Thanks to Mrs. Gaskell and the myth the tourists came and came— more than ten thousand already in 1895, and a string of guidebooks followed to guide them on the trail. The incumbent of the parsonage who came after Patrick Brontë replaced the old windows and did the usual upgrades, including a new wing for the house. He also knocked down and rebuilt the church, to the annoyance of the already growing band of Brontë fans. He also put up a screen of trees to block the stream of gawpers into his front room, and refused admission for the increasingly insistent and intrusive tourists. It must have been pretty horrid for him, trying to do his job as a vicar and maintain some privacy. . . . If you had visited the parsonage in 1900, you would have had to do a good deal more imagining than now. But in 1927 the parsonage was bought for the Brontë Society by a local bigwig, and the house was preserved as a museum. In the 1950s it was restored to its former clean but dark majesty and decorated in authentic style based on old pictures. The back-construction of Haworth is physical as well as imaginative.

I have spent a lot of time in Jerusalem at sites of religious pilgrimage that are not only back-constructions but back-constructions of things that never happened and certainly didn't happen there. I still find it weird watching pilgrims intently kissing the ground of the route of the Stations of the Cross, when we know that the ground Jesus walked is many feet below the current level, that most of the stations are based on fabricated medieval stories, and that even if Jesus did go from court to crucifixion at the site memorialized by the Church of the Holy Sepulchre this was not the route. But I have also learned that powerful feelings aren't often swayed by academics yelling about fakes and truth. Deriding relics and other people's sacred rites has been good sport for centuries, but it is far more interesting to think about why we all need our pilgrimages. Haworth isn't quite like the Stations of the Cross, but it is worth asking why it continues to have such a pull on the imagination.

"Darling!" said my wife, with a certain exasperation, "It's girl stuff." That must be true. Charlotte Brontë is the story of the girl who struggled to find a voice, who epitomizes the difficulties of becoming a writer as a woman, then, of course, but still now. Haworth stands for every woman's home, the repression of the inner self in social propriety—and Charlotte's need to use a man's name to publish at first demonstrates the social constraints against which she fights, just as *Jane Eyre* is the story of a girl's journey into self-assertion, a pilgrimage in itself. Haworth is the symbol of a woman's struggle for self-expression. "Darling!" said my wife, the family lawyer. "Fathers? Brothers?" And just before I could say "the personal is political," I recognized that in any argument about girl stuff there are moments for a relentlessly male academic to keep quiet, and that it was obviously right also that there are some great archetypes for the family romance in the bullying father who did not know his daughters were writing, and who tried to prevent his daughter from marrying, and in the talented brother, the chosen one, destined for failure and self-destruction. Surviving the family is *the* modern narrative, the biography everyone shares.

Haworth lets us tell some stories that have a real cultural power. That's how these pilgrimage sites work, I think. The site has a pull on our imagination because it can stimulate stories of real cultural richness, stories that embody our innermost concerns. And here, half way between Scott and Freud, our profound need to understand family dynamics, the search for self-expression and creativity, and the conflicts of gender, keep us coming back to Haworth.

It isn't just tourists on a wet Sunday, either. After Mrs. Gaskell, there have been hundreds of biographies of each member of the Brontë family and of the family together. There seems to be a particular obsessiveness when it comes to the biographical pursuit of the Brontës, even in comparison with other biographers. In the 1960s the prizewinning accounts were written by Winifred Gérin, who eventually received an OBE from the queen for her efforts. She was an English woman who married a Belgian poet and cellist, who died young; after this, she lived for ten years with her sister, a painter, before marrying again, this time to a biographer of Patrick Brontë whom she met at Haworth. She had already written a play about Charlotte's attachment to her Belgian tutor. She went on to publish separate biographies of the four Brontë children, and then of Mrs. Gaskell.

Gérin moved to Haworth to get closer to her subjects: "Living in Haworth," she explained, "has allowed me to see Branwell's world—both the inner and the outer—with something of the permanence that underlies the seasons' changes." I have "been to every place where he lived or worked; in many cases found the actual houses in which he lodged or which he visited; and met the descendents of the people who were his friends or employers"—this, more than a hundred and twenty years after Branwell worked in a railway office! Why would you want to meet the great-grandchildren of even your own great-grandfather's boss? The same with Anne: "I have followed her everywhere to see what she saw," pursuing "every available trail" . . . "even to the humblest relic." It gets almost creepy, like a stalker. "I could not rest," she confesses, "till I had removed the tangle of ivy and bramble" from the neglected grave of—Anne's *schoolteacher*. Her conclusion gives Haworth itself an almost mystical power, the key to uncovering the truth of the Brontës' characters: "When all has been visited it is from Haworth itself that the most can be learnt about the Brontës."

So much for the books. The fascination with the Brontës bites deep and leads the biographer to walk in every footstep, to collect every discarded tchotchke as a relic (Anne's *teapot* is "a silent witness" to her true character! I ask you . . .), and to believe that you can get to their inner world by living where they lived. The only other place you see language like this is with religious pilgrims. At this level, going to Haworth feels like joining a cult.

The weather, at least, delivered. We arrived from Keighley in mist, rain, and wind, and glowering storm clouds, when the mist lifted enough to see them—and this was late May. "There is always a north-westerly here," said the owner of our bed and breakfast. "In winter, this is the coldest place on earth." The Brontë wind, which appears in every story of Haworth, forcing the girls inside to huddle round the fire, rattling the windows, carrying away the words of lovers, still blows . . . and gusted all the time we were there. Even so, the moors were plush rather than grim, with flowering gorse, Henry Moore wind-turned rocks, and fat sheep with lambs pushing hard into their mothers' teats, tails shaking wildly. The gray stone houses press up together against the weather with pretty little gardens and flat dark windows. The fields are ordered with well-kept dry-stone walls. Hardly a mysterious stunted tree or ruined hall in sight.

The first surprise is the sheer size of Haworth. There is inevitably some modern development, but the town's Victorian buildings dominate as you go up the hill from the old railway station toward the parsonage. To read Mrs. Gaskell you might imagine a tiny hamlet on a hilltop, deserted and surrounded, even threatened, by the moors around. But Haworth is a decent-size place; it had nearly seven thousand inhabitants in 1850, with three mills at its industrial center. It did not experience the fearsome growth of nearby Bradford, which swelled from ten thousand to over a hundred thousand between 1800 and 1850, but it spreads up and down and around the hill: the solitude of the Brontë sisters seems to have been partly an issue of class, partly of willfulness. There are signs of old mills and current small industry on the hills around Haworth too. Keighley, a medium-size town with a professional rugby team, is four miles away; Bradford a dozen. If you came from the Midwest of the United States where the vast flat lands offer desolate distances of a magnitude undreamt of by these Victorian ladies, Haworth is positively teeming.

The main street, which leads up to the parsonage, is startlingly steep, with thick cobbles, and dark gray-red stone cottages on each side. Theocritus, the hypersophisticated Greek pastoral poet, says "You could not fail to recognize Lycidas for a shepherd, because he looked exactly like one." Well, this street looks exactly like a Victorian Yorkshire street. The cottages are four-square, solidly built in stone, with doors that open straight onto the pavement. There are some shops with mullioned bow windows. There is, even in May, a smell of domestic fires, mingling with the damp of the mist and the peaty, heathery whiff of the moors beyond. Everyone has to trudge, huddled over, up the steepness, as in a Lowrie painting. This was the street up which the horses labored with the Brontës' luggage, with their hooves in cloths to give better traction against the cobbles. Except that now every second house is a bed and breakfast; there are jolly cake shops, and in front of us a tour of thirty Japanese schoolgirls giggling and pointing. If de Quincey and his servant were freaked out by a Malay in the Lake District, it is hard to imagine what Emily would have made of a crocodile of Japanese girls coming up the parsonage path. Haworth is probably the only parish church in Britain with signs in Japanese.

The parsonage is still very clean. The pathway up to the front door is spotless; the little garden in front is pretty and has no leaf out of place; the front step still scoured. Every room is tidy, neat, and anti-septic. The hall is narrow, but its stone floor is polished smooth. This is not the cleanliness of moral approbation, though, just the health and safety of institutional preservation. To the right is Patrick Brontë's study, where he sat, going blind, taking his meals alone, and grumpily directing his children's lives. To the left, the dining room, where the girls sat at the table and wrote. The rooms are cramped, even after the extensions: both rooms too small for a king-size bed and two fat people getting dressed. From the outside, the house looks rather grand. Victorian parsonages are now very desirable properties, often, as here, one of the largest houses in the village. But inside Haworth Parsonage, things feel too constrained for comfort, especially for a family of seven. The visitors are kept behind ropes just inside the doors of the rooms. Mrs. Gaskell, on her first visit—we all do this—had taken a good look at the books on the shelves in the dining room. ("No standard reading" was her conclusion. What better badge of honor than to have one's reading thought out of the ordinary by a famous writer?) The books now are hard to see because you aren't allowed into the room, but it isn't the Brontës' own collection. I could make out the *Cornhill Magazine* on the top shelf, which is a fair choice: the Brontës did read contemporary journals avidly. On the bottom were heavy bound volumes of the Brontë Society—which I suppose had to be put somewhere. Harriet Martineau, a feminist herself who should have known better, started the idea that the Haworth Parsonage was somehow outside the literary currents of the time. "This was a place where newspapers were never seen," she wrote. But the Brontës devoured Scott and Lockhart and Byron and Bulwer Lytton and Thackeray, all the up-to-date, trendy figures, and studied the journals in which their work was discussed too. It's mildly disappointing, if wholly understandable, that the books today look like random furnishings for a generalized Victorian effect.

The parsonage tries to do two things at once. It wants to give a sense of the house as it was lived in: so we have the dining room with its books and a table with little objects from the sisters on it. "This is where it all happened . . ." But it also is a museum. So upstairs there are items in glass cases and a display of the Brontë history, which is detailed and well laid out. It's an awkward mix. (Dove Cottage gets round it better by having the museum quite separate from the house.) The children's study, where Emily lay on the couch by the window and looked out at the wind, is a tiny cupboard of a space and intensely evocative just because it is so small, like the dens we made as kids, only too square and undecorated to feel really cozy. But in the middle of

Emily's bedroom in Haworth Parsonage: the sheer smallness of the space evokes the intense intimacy of a child's den.

Charlotte's bedroom is a glass-fronted cabinet with some of her clothes in it—a dress, a pair of shoes, and a rather faded cream stocking with a hole near the top of the thigh. What Victorian woman, let alone the cripplingly shy Charlotte, would want her used underwear on display? The caps, especially the wedding hat, were cute lacy numbers (I was assured by Helen and my wife). But looking at collections behind glass is a very different experience from nosing around a house to sense how someone lived. The exhibition was a good example of modern exhibition skills, with some great artifacts: the little books the Brontës had composed as children, with microscopic writing and illustrations; Charlotte's trunk, which she had used in Belgium; some fascinating manuscripts. But as David commented, it was far more moving— heart-stopping—for him to see the actual autograph manuscript of *Jane Eyre*, in the British Library, open to the page where Charlotte had written, "Reader, I married him," that first physical inscription of one of the iconic statements of fiction, than to see all of Charlotte's underwear and hats. The house, much redesigned and without the mundane touches and serendipities of everyday collisions that make a space feel lived-in, was unemotive, unexpressive. Between the glass cabinets and the roped-off rooms, the parsonage felt soulless.

There were two moments, though, that stopped me in my tracks and changed the way I felt about the everyday of Haworth Parsonage. The first was discovering that the room where the beloved servant Tabby had lived originally had its own outside entrance and was blocked off from the rest of the house. The servants' quarters, even for a financially insecure parson, and even when the single servant was by all written accounts made to feel so much a part of the family, nonetheless forced "dear Tabby" to go out into the wind and rain and back through the downstairs door to join the others, always, even at night. The physicality of class in Victorian Britain is emphatic. The second was learning that the Brontës had a classy two-seater privy outside. Now, outdoor privies were still normal, and the Babbage report, which picked out Haworth as particularly unsanitary, complained that most families had to share a single privy with four other families. But the parsonage had a private two-seater. It opened visions of Anne and Emily taking their makeup and going out together for a gossip and a pee. Haworth lightened up.

The parsonage has a graveyard—*the* graveyard—pressing in at the end of the short garden. And what an amazing graveyard it is! It has a canopy of massive trees from which crows cawed loudly into the wind, and the gravestones themselves are all huge, much larger than usual headstones, and packed in tightly. Some are laid flat on risers, like tables, altars of strange cults. Others, too close together to read the names, lean into the wind, against the slope of the land, a dense palisade of signs of the dead. There are no grass borders, no flowers, and the shadow from the trees and the black soil between the gray-green, weighty memorials, give the scene a darkness that was easy to imagine seeping into the Brontës' writing. Death was all too insistently familiar to Haworth: over 41 percent of children died before they were six years old, and there are incredibly twenty thousand burials in what is a small, walled cemetery. Old Patrick Brontë buried many hundreds of children apart from his own. The church and the graveyard fill the view through the front windows of the parsonage, as the moors fill the back. The trees were planted only after the Brontës had left, however. Back then on sunny days the women of the village had used the gravestones to dry their washing on; Reverend Nichols, years before he became Charlotte's husband, was annoyed by such flippancy and angrily evicted the women—to the amusement of Patrick Brontë, at a time when he could still just about see the graves and his four children. There is something touchingly fitting to the painful banality of Victorian working life in the earnest curate's anger at the washerwomen's earthy combination of death and laundry.

Thousands visit the Brontë Museum in Brontë country. In May there were school trips from France, busily adding to workbooks, and tour groups from Japan, snapping away intently; English families, with bored children; elderly couples, with slow pace, wondering aloud about Emily in the kitchen and Charlotte's possible pregnancy. None followed us into the graveyard. But by 5:30, even on a Saturday night in late spring, Haworth suddenly and bafflingly looked empty. The shops were shut and the pubs silent. By the time we went to dinner the streets were completely deserted, except for two snively youths under a lamppost smoking. After the bustle of the day, the town seemed eerily lonely and darkening: the Brontë effect, I guess. We quickly became the four soft southerners: "Better to live in total isolation in a hut in

Haworth Parsonage from the graveyard: I "wondered how anyone could ever imagine unquiet slumbers, for the sleepers in that quiet earth," Emily Brontë.

Norway like Wittgenstein," said David in his best Schopenhauerian tones. "What do you do without concerts and movies and theater and sushi?" I shuddered. We drove off to a country house hotel to eat, a redbrick Jacobean building, which loomed dripping out of the mist, with fairy lights in the garden trees.

The only other people in the bar were three sharply dressed young women waiting for lost friends. "Use your tom-tom," said one into her mobile in the broadest of Yorkshire accents, and then "Inshallah, inshallah." (I didn't know a tom-tom was a GPS device, but everyone else seemed to.) Four Jews, three Muslims, meet in a Jacobean hotel in Yorkshire and . . . the waitress prevented any joke developing by bringing the wine list. "I'll give you two minutes to make your choice," she said, making it sound like an ultimatum. What makes for local culture is changing in Britain, as it is in so many places across the world. This change—an effect and symptom, I suppose, of contemporary globalization—alters how pilgrimage works today. Here we were, Hebrews and Musulmen, as the Victorians would have put it in outraged tones, and the three young women unchaperoned, at that, comfortably ensconced as guests in what was once the manor house, the center of the estate—and the scene of so many Victorian novels. It was now a hotel with food that looked like food you could get in pretty well any town in Europe (pan-fried salmon with lemon-butter and spinach). Most pilgrimages have their food story—the struggle with local produce, the comfort of the last piece of chocolate from home. All we had was the Good Food Guide and a credit card. The culture clash we felt up north on a wet Saturday in deserted Haworth was nothing compared to the great pilgrimages of the past, where the road to Jerusalem took medieval Englishmen through increasingly shocking and exotic challenges of foreignness. The crusaders massacred Eastern Christians along with the infidels because they couldn't recognize them as Christians like themselves at all. Getting lost on the moors now was solved by the tom-tom, and the Jews and the Muslims acknowledged each other across cocktails.

Haworth is a site of international tourism, where every visitor is led to look at the otherness of the past, the Brontës' past, from their own perspectives—as schoolchildren packaged through culture, as lovers of the novels, as searchers after Britain's quaintness, as a family on a day out, and so forth. As in all museums, part of the process is watching the other visitors. Everyone is engaged in a small drama of self-definition. Haworth is an especially good place for this. From the beginning, the Brontës have put forward a particular combination of ordinariness and exceptionality—in a quite different way from Scott, the Wizard of the North, or Wordsworth, the Sage of the Lakes. The Brontës at one level were desperate to appear ordinary—rather than to be stared at as coarse or strange or famous. The house cherishes the games of the children, sisters and brother making up stories together, making bread in the kitchen, the everyday life of domestic chores interspersed with writing—as so many young women did write their journals, their poetry, their stories in their own normal houses. The Brontës are a recognizable, miserable family. At the same time, the house proclaims the exceptionality of these children. These children's childish microscopic stories grew into novels that sit firmly at the center of the Western canon. These sisters died young like James Dean; here is the cradle of genius, strange and famous. What were the Brontës like? That's the question of Haworth. But as we look round, it is always also a question of what we are like, how we imagine ourselves—how ordinary, how exceptional, how local, how international, how (un)like the family inside, how (un)like the lonely, inward girls, back from school, writing in the parsonage . . .

Our waitress was not like any other waitress I had ever come across, though. I had never encountered a waitress who had full-on hiccups and tried to go through with the whole waitress spiel anyway: "Who is—*hic*—having the sar—*hic*—dines?" "Can I—*hic*—get you any coff—*hic*—ee or—*hic*—tea?" Our attempts at sympathetic smiles at this Dickensian high comedy were rebuffed blankly: with stony and stolid sangfroid, she proceeded through her duties without once acknowledging there was anything untoward. The little irruptions of the uncontrollable real of her body totally derailed the conventionality of her job. In a comedy, acted, it would feel like a labored bit of slapstick. In a would-be upmarket restaurant it played pretty riotously to us. There isn't much giggling in the Brontë myth, and the real easily gets lost, the more the museum and the myth claim to serve it up.

We walked the moors next day in blustery sunshine: brisk, head-clearing, unromantic. You can't do Haworth without the moors, without at least imagining yourself shouting "Cathy!" into the storm or staring moodily at the Brontë waterfall (which isn't quite the cataract we had hoped for). Like Hazlitt, David likes to walk untalking; my wife, the family lawyer, chatted about her cases, exceptionally unhappy normal families. Haworth was better to imagine than to visit, I reflected, as I stared back across the valley, eyes watering in the wind. With "Haworth" as a place in the Brontë myth, I could summon up the darkness of a home life stunted by circumstance, the soaring reach of the imagination grasping at a fulfilled internal life, and turning to us with an affirmative "Reader, I married him" against the impediments of a limiting and oppressive existence. But in the actual house itself, we get showcased the relic of a holy stocking in a cabinet.

For the first time, I think I understand one part of why pilgrims kiss relics, and bloody their knees to approach a grave, and lie crying on the floor. The sheer physicality brings you into direct contact with something essentially material, whatever other spiritualities or fantasies are in play. In the parsonage, nothing can be touched—and nothing was particularly touching. It was all too clean. The real behind glass. Without any grit, without the feel of such materiality, the house had lost its soul as a lived-in space.

What is on offer in this our current culture of display, it seems, is not the messy real of a writer's inhabited world, in which you can imagine the personal creation of great art. Instead, you get fragments of an artist's material life set in rooms that are part museum, part the real thing. A virtual display. Can we tell if it really is Charlotte's trunk? Would it change our reactions if it were an unannounced replica? What is celebrated is an amorphous sense of literature as English heritage: the Victorian novels as signs of our grand past, like stately homes and top hats. As with Abbotsford, visits to Haworth go up when it is raining: it is a place indoors to visit in a worthwhile sort of way, with a touch of piety, and the comfortable feel of tea-towels and pencils in the heritage-themed shop. If I am becoming more sympathetic toward the Victorian pilgrims' sense of where writers come from, I think I am becoming even more disenchanted with its modern reperformances. The Brontë myth, I decided as we left Haworth, like all myths, works best when it takes up residence in the imagination.

5

OH FOR A MUSE OF FIRE!

URING MY FINAL two years of high school, I saw almost every play put on in London, from the profundities at the Old Vic to the student experiments at the Young Vic—though, with my adolescent intellectualism in full flight, I scornfully spurned what we called the tourist plays—the most gaudy musicals and, with a special sniffiness, *The Mousetrap* (which I still haven't seen). Weekends in the hills alternated with weekends on Shaftesbury Avenue, without any sense of conflict, although my literary friends for the theater trips, trainee bitchy critics all, were very different from my hairy friends for the mountains. You could buy tickets cheaply, I was prepared to stand, and, since I saw everything, I was there for dramas destined to become legendary events, as I occasionally realized at the time, and plenty of shows that were disasters or, even worse, just mediocre. The lure of the theater was why my first road trip was to Stratford-upon-Avon.

Everyone remembers their first road trip. I don't mean the first time you go away with your family, or the first time you go away with your school. I mean the first time you get in a car with just your friends and drive off, to the sound of your parents' anxiety, on an adventure. Hollywood has helped make it a paradigm of the journey of self-discovery, or a parody of it. In my case, it was a friend's old Mini, two nights in a hotel with garish, lobster-themed décor, and the complete history plays at Stratford. And, with the usual mixture of bravado and insecurity, we hung around in the pub afterward, the Dirty Duck, catching sights of the actors, who were, of course, far too cool even half to notice some intense, intellectual, stagestruck teenagers (who are presumably always there, like the actors).

My favorite description of a life-changing, mesmerizing trip to the theater is from yet another bookish and obsessive hero of mine, Marcel Proust, one of the least likely heroes to appear in a book on pilgrimage, granted he spent his last years in a cork-lined study refusing even to leave his dead mother's house. The narrator of *A la recherche du temps perdu* tells a funny and moving story of his youth. He knows he is going to hear the great actress Rachel perform in a tragedy. So he gets a copy of the play and practices reading the heroine's great speech. He tries it with this intonation and that emphasis and this gesture, till he feels he has covered all the possibilities. He strides to the theater with the confidence he will be observing which of his options Rachel will choose. When he hears her, however, he is completely blown away by a language, thought, and passion that he could not imagine before, and finds himself emotionally overwhelmed. That's how it can be with the great Shakespearean performances. You can be reduced to helplessness by the eruption of laughter at a line you thought you knew, or by the welling of tears at a speech whose emotional range you were sure you had mapped. A whole play can be revisioned. For me, seeing great Shakespearean actors for the first time at Stratford took school texts and turned them into revelatory masterpieces.

Now, I was about to write an unfortunate sentence about the place of Shakespeare in education in Britain—a topic that hits the letters pages of the English newspapers about once a decade, with the usual barmy muddle of nostalgia, ignorance, and nationalist fantasy—when my wife put me straight: you can do Shakespeare without the full postcolonial crisis of facing up to Englishness. "Shakespeare at school?" she said calmly. "Why not?" Americans, she explained, can hunt down the Great American Novel—*The Great Gatsby* or *Catcher in the Rye* are read by just about everyone who gets an education worth the name, with *Moby Dick* for the more ambitious and Hemingway for the more macho, or Toni Morrison for the more modern—and you can do the Great American Play too, like *Death of a Salesman*, but thanks to the general melting-pot principle (and so forth), you don't have to put your national identity on the line every time you choose a play to read in class. "And what's so wrong with musicals, anyway?"

She has a point, of course (even about musicals: Bing Crosby is now the height of retro chic, and Hoagy Carmichael the cool, cool, cool of any evening). Nonetheless, for us Brits, Shakespeare is inevitably a statue as well as a book: he's become a national icon, a speech writer for flag-waving patriots, a figure who captures the essence of what it is to be really English: "He is central to the centre, the core or source of Englishness itself," as one celebrated modern biographer puts it, with a disturbingly unreflective jingoism. And that has really changed Stratford-upon-Avon too: it has become the birthplace of English genius. The Elizabethan period, the home of Merrie England, with all those half-timbered houses, ruffed heads, and virgin queens, has become a quintessential moment of Englishness in English history, in a way the seventeenth century, despite the decapitation of Charles I, has never quite managed (not to mention the thirteenth or fourteenth centuries, which are horrid even for historians). The combination of empire-building and heroic adventurers like Sir Francis Drake helped too, probably. Stratford has been on the tourist trail for a long time now.

But it is, once again, the Victorians who are really to blame for Stratford's fate. Shakespeare had retired quietly to Stratford and a life as a property owner, when he died. He is buried in the church there, not in Westminster Abbey in Poets' Corner (although there is now a bust to memorialize him with the other greats of literature), and his passing away was not a national moment at all. There were no great outpourings of grief à la Princess Diana. His death was barely noted. For the next hundred and fifty years, his plays had their ups and downs, rewritten to suit the taste of the moment, usually with a regrettably happier endings for the few tragedies that were performed. The man himself was not of great interest, and Stratford was barely on the map. It all began to change when the great eighteenth-century actor Garrick decided to grace a jubilee celebration of Shakespeare in Stratford, an attempt by local burghers to raise some money for the town. The town then had fewer than six hundred houses and a population around three thousand. It was not easy to reach, and there was, of course, no public transport.

The jubilee took place in 1769 (not an actual jubilee year, but the thought is what counts). There were guns on the riverbank to fire a salute, there were speeches and presentations, and there were songs and poems recited. There was some excitement about the ribbon specially woven for the event, to be worn by all the participants, and about the medal struck for Garrick to wear on his ribbon. There was a local crowd and visitors from London and the surrounding towns. Typically, it rained and rained, and the roads descended into mud pits. The inns were all overbooked and prices skyrocketed—asked for the time, one canny local apparently asked a shilling to tell a stranger the hour, and then asked for extra pennies to add the minutes. Garrick's poetry, somewhat laughably to modern ears, luxuriantly praised "Avonian Willy." But to modern eyes, the weirdest thing about the celebration was that no plays of Shakespeare were performed. There was no theater at Stratford, either. This was a mixture of grand parade and soaking civic ceremony—not a festival of drama.

Looking back from the nineteenth century, however, Garrick seemed to be the start of something big. Throughout the Victorian era, there were further, far grander jubilees celebrated, most splendidly in 1864. This time they staged plays in a temporary theater, as well as holding glorious and expensive dinners for grandees. There were fireworks and, since this was mid-Victorian earnestness, sermons preached on Sunday by the Archbishop of Dublin and the Bishop of Saint Andrew's. There was even a performance of Handel's *Messiah*, the classic musical demonstration of Victorian national bonding, which has lasted into modern England too. (Even for a Jewish boy, it was weird when we went to hear the *Messiah* in King's College Chapel, and my wife, the New Yorker, couldn't sing along under her breath—or didn't find my humming a bonding moment, at any rate.) There were arguments for some years before the jubilee whether London or Stratford was the right place for such an event, now explicitly taken as a symbolic display of empire. The advertising included train times and prices (second-class round-trip from Cambridge was twenty shillings, surprisingly high). For four pence you could buy through the post an ode on the three hundreth birthday of Shakespeare by Martin Tupper, Queen Victoria's favorite poet; and Rock Brothers and Payne produced a charming aide-memoir of the occasion called *The Home of Shakespeare.*

The jubilee of 1864 shows how rapidly things had changed in Britain since Garrick's day, with trains replacing horses, newspapers and journals spreading the word across the country, and the imperial significance of the event proclaimed by its national committee. But underlying all this, Shakespeare himself had changed. Thomas Carlyle as ever sets the new tone. Here is how Shakespeare emerges as a hero—and fit for hero worship—in Carlyle's inimitable prose: "We can fancy him as radiant aloft over all Nations of Englishmen, a thousand years hence. From Paramatta, from New York, wheresoever, under whatever sort of Parish-Constable so ever, English men and women are, they will say to one another, 'Yes this Shakespeare is ours; we produced him, we speak and think by him; we are of one blood and kind with him.'" For the Victorians, in search of a national identity to match the national project of empire and rule, Shakespeare had become the national poet—like Homer for the Greeks, a figurehead whose words, shared, learned, loved, would act as a glue to bond Englishmen wherever they might be, on a map where, for Carlyle, New York is as outlandish as Paramatta, where the pink of the British Empire stretches across the globe. This Victorian Shakespeare, Shakespeare as a national heritage, is dying only slowly—which is why every few years the English media get into a tizzy about "compulsory Shakespeare" in schools.

It was the Victorians who found Shakespeare's birthplace and made it a shrine of pilgrimage. Although there is one eighteenth-century map with "the house where Shakespeare was born" on it, the house now visited as Shakespeare's birthplace was sold in 1805, and the handbill advertising the sale did not mention any connection to Shakespeare. It was a pub, the Swan and Maidenhead, and sold as a going business. In 1806 R. B. Wheler, a local bigwig, published his book called *History and Antiquities of Stratford-upon-Avon*. This contains an engraving of the house, still with its pub sign, but no mention in the text of any significant connection between it and Shakespeare. In 1824, however, W. Moncrief described his visit, with directions—by horse—and comments that the "humble shed, in which the immortal bard first drew breath . . . is still existing." He adds tellingly: "All who have a heart to feel and a mind to admire the truth of nature and the splendour of genius, will rush thither to behold it, as a pilgrim would to the shrine of some loved saint; will deem it holy ground, and dwell with sweet though pensive rapture on the natal habitation of the poet." An American called Jones gave a jubilee oration in Stratford in 1836. He came, he declared, as "the Pilgrim at the Poetic Shrine of his Native land" (he had emigrated to America), and reflected: "The humblest cottage of Stratford first echoed his infant cries; yet is that lowly dwelling to the poetic pilgrim far more dear than the sceptred palace." A gushing poem by Mrs. Elvington tells you exactly how religiously to feel: "With sacred awe I gaze these walls around And tread with rev'rence o'er this hallowed ground . . ." The house—a humble shed, like the manger of Jesus—has become a temple to the national bard, a religious memorial of English genius and character. A site of pilgrimage.

When Shakespeare's father died he owned the two houses in Henley Street now known as Shakespeare's birthplace. He bought the first, the Town Records show, in 1556. There is no direct evidence he owned the other—where Shakespeare is said to have been born—until 1575, well after William's birth, though he may have rented it for some time before, or even purchased it earlier. The houses have undergone substantial renovation over the years and in 1769 looked quite different from now and from their Elizabethan architecture. It was in the Victorian period that the house was restored to its "Elizabethan look," based on an eighteenth-century engraving, though in the earlier days it had stood in a line of houses, and now it is detached for greater visual drama. The official program of the 1864 tercentenary celebrations announced that the house was "a relic worthy of being preserved by a nation grateful for the perpetuation and enrichment of its language." The auction poster in 1847 offered the house as "the truly heart-stirring relic of a most glorious period and of England's immortal bard." But only the cellar of the birthplace house and the bare structural shape of the rooms is fully Elizabethan. Halliwell-Phillipps, who wrote the standard Victorian biography of Shakespeare, smartly sidesteps any doubts about the status of "the relic" by declaring that Shakespeare's birthplace has been identified "through unvarying tradition," and consequently it would be "the merest foppery of scepticism to doubt that it is the apartment now exhibited as the birth-place." R. E. Hunter, the secretary of the committee for the tercentenary celebrations in 1864, agreed: "'Tradition' remarks Mr Knight, 'says that Shakespeare was born in one of the houses in Henley Street; tradition points to the very room in which he was born. Let us not disturb the belief'. To disturb it is impossible, and the author should have said—

'We could not if we would
And would not if we could'."

Both Halliwell-Phillipps and Hunter, as they hint, knew well enough how difficult it actually was to pin down the very room, or to declare that the very room was actually Elizabethan. It seems to have been Garrick, with his flair for dramatization, who first pointed out the "very birth-place." But, for the biographer and the organizer of the celebration, tradition was on their economic and ideological side. The room's window has scratched into it the signatures of Walter Scott, Thomas Carlyle, Tennyson, Keats, Longfellow, Harriet Beecher Stowe . . . all paying their respects with a little piece of memorialization of their own. The visits by great artists to the shrine of the great artist have become part of the tour, as tradition builds up its own history, its own momentum.

The tourist industry is more than usually exposed by Stratford. There is a story that Shakespeare planted a mulberry tree at New

Place. The tree, Shakespeare's or no, was cut down in 1750 by its owner, irate at the first tourists to the shrine, and the wood was bought by an enterprising businessman, aptly called Sharp. He began to make relics from the wood and sell them. When Garrick was made a freeman of the borough during the first jubilee, he was presented with his deed "in a small, neat chest, constructed from a mulberry tree planted by Shakespeare himself." (He thanked them officially for the "elegant and inestimable box.") Thousands of objects were produced and sold over the years, so that Sharp felt forced on his deathbed to take an oath that every single one was an authentic piece of Shakespeare's tree. As one gentle and amused commentator notes: "It would be unkind to think of perjury in the case of Thomas Sharp. . . . We can only conclude that it was a very big tree indeed."

Relics have been on sale in Stratford ever since. In the nineteenth century Shakespeare's chair was sold several times, in pieces and whole, by another unscrupulous (or imaginative) saleswoman. The best forgeries have been manuscripts, with a flourishing nineteenth-century trade in personal letters and new plays, some of which survived a few years before being revealed as fakes. The difficulty is that the facts known about Shakespeare's life could be written on a single sheet of paper—the innumerable biographies are full of giveaway phrases such as "must have," "probably," "surely," to cover the padding—and the more the poet became the Bard of the Nation, the blessed guardian of the English language, the more people wanted to envisage a life that matched the role. The Victorians, fascinated with the lives and personalities of authors, *had* to have a biography of Shakespeare. The anecdotes and the relics multiplied to meet the need.

Even so, it is a remarkable sign of the religious awe with which writers and their houses are invested, and the spirit of pilgrimage with which they are visited, that this spot managed to evoke such emotional responses from its Victorian tourists, English and American alike. Shakespeare wrote most of his plays and performed all of his roles in London. He left Stratford—as soon as he could?—to get to where the theater was. What we are all asked to do at Stratford is to believe that a birthplace somehow affects a poet's future life as a writer in a significant way: "A visit to this old house . . . bewilders the mind with 'thick-coming fancies' of Shakespeare's 'mewling infancy', child-hood innocence, and studious boyhood," as one Victorian lovingly enthused. I just don't get how any birthplace, or even a schoolroom, could have such a mystique. "Perhaps as a boy he may have sat in the corner feasting his galloping imagination from a spark in the ashes." Perhaps. I care about lots of writers, but I don't know the houses where any of them were born, nor can I imagine that it would make a difference to me if I did. I haven't visited my own birthplace either. But for Washington Irving—and he is typical in this—even when he knows the touristy side of things is ridiculous, he cannot help being seriously affected by walking where Shakespeare walked, and stand-ing over the bard's tomb. He feels the presence of greatness. It was for this he came to England.

Stratford held a particular attraction for American visitors in the Victorian period. John Adams and Thomas Jefferson, two future presi-dents of the United States, visited Stratford together in 1786, and they were followed by a constant stream of visitors in the nineteenth century. Andrew Carnegie funded the building of the town's library. There is a window in the church, "the gift of America to Shakespeare's church," unveiled by the American ambassador in 1896. Mark Twain described his trip to Stratford, constantly menaced by Marie Corelli, as the worst day of his whole life. Shakespeare maintained an extraordinary place in American cultural life in the nineteenth century—perhaps most vividly captured by the Astor Place Riot. In 1849 thirty-one people were killed and more than a hundred and fifty injured in a riot at the Astor Place Theatre in New York during a performance of *Macbeth*, a riot that pitted the supporters of Macready, the great English touring actor and friend of Dickens, against those of Forrest, the great Ameri-can Shakespearean star. American soldiers fired on American citizens to protect the theater. The battle was more about class, power, and anti-English feeling than simple differences of aesthetic principle, but it is not by chance that it took place at a performance of Shakespeare.

Shakespeare was read and performed by all classes. A Californian newspaper in 1857 wrote, "There is hardly a butcher or a newspaper boy in the city who does not understand 'like a book,' the majority of the playable plays of Shakespeare, so often have they seen them acted, ranted, or slaughtered upon our boards." De Tocqueville, in his famous journey of discovery round America, was amazed to find copies of Shakespeare in rural shacks. Mark Twain remembered the master of the steamboat reading Shakespeare to him as a young apprentice, "not just casually but by the hour. . . . He did not use the book, and did not need to; he knew his Shakespeare as well as Euclid ever knew his multiplication table." Although cowboy films keep showing the same image of the western saloon, the diggers of the Gold Rush were heavily into their Shakespeare on the long winter nights. Shakespeare was owned by Americans in a way that no other work of English literature was—and thus could become a site for cultural warfare like no other performance. He was, as James Fenimore Cooper crowed, our countryman, an American. Nowadays, tens of thousands of Americans a year process through Shakespeare's house, which is one of the fixed points on the cultural tour of England, between Oxford and Bath.

The walk up from the station to Shakespeare's birthplace is rather dispiriting. Stratford was not bombed during the Second World War, unlike nearby Coventry and Birmingham, but the town certainly shows the horrors of modern urban development to the full: major roads slicing through an old town, shopping centers flattening old quarters for modern, neon-lit boxes, the same chain shops as any other town. Not so much the center of Englishness as middle England writ large. Almost everywhere screams Shakespeare: the Othello Bistro; Hamlet Way (a dead end, inevitably); the Anne Hathaway Tea Rooms. (We started a name game immediately: Titus Andronicus butchers? Ophelia swimming pool? Goneril and Regan Real Estate?) Henley Street itself, however, where Shakespeare's birthplace is located, is a uniquely unpleasant combination of paraded olden times and commercialized modern squalor. It is now a broad pedestrian area, far wider than any Elizabethan thoroughfare. On one side of the street, there are cafés and garish souvenir shops. In May, one was unaccountably full of large Father Christmas dolls. Tourists mill around and snap photographs. Shakespeare's house, clean and restored, is at the center of the other side of the street. It stands out because the houses on either side were destroyed by the Victorian planners—in the same way as they destroyed the medieval houses in front of King's College, Cambridge, to create another famous tourist view. Black iron railings and luxuriant flowers keep everyone from the front of the house (everyone now has to use the back door). It has the timbers exposed, as one would expect for an Elizabethan house—though this effect was also created by the Victorian restoration, as the frontage had been bricked over in the eighteenth century. There are three gables with windows in the roof, pleasingly arranged asymmetrically. Again, these are Victorian reconstructions, based on old pictures; the roof in the eighteenth century was unbroken. Above the door to the right is a glass panel that shows off the wattle and daub with which the house would have been built: it exhibits the site's constructedness, a piece of didactic tourism, a flash of the authentic beneath (under some very inauthentic display glass). Above the gabled door itself is a wholly modern shield with a fake coat of arms made out of a nibbed pen. Presumably this fits someone's sense of Elizabethan imagery. Shakespeare's father was fined for having a large and foul dung heap outside his door. This is a very clean site.

To the left of the house, and never included in the photographs of it, is the Shakespeare Centre, the only way now into the birthplace and its garden. This is a very ugly 1960s concrete building, with a new entrance hall for the tourists. (The house on the other side is old and rather beautiful—preserved thanks to Marie Corelli's insistent interference with the Victorian town council's plans.) The route in is carefully managed. After the ticket booth, three rooms with videos and displays of increasingly grotesque vulgarity process the visitor into the lovely gardens. "Your journey into Shakespeare's house starts here," proclaims the first screen with a disconcerting lack of truth—and promptly turns into a performance of the prologue from *Henry V*:

"Oh for a muse of fire . . ." (and we will need every invocation of a muse of the imagination for what follows). The second room has fake grass, a horrid pastoral scene painted on the wall, and spotlights used to illuminate objects from an Elizabethan schoolroom—though too quickly for anyone to look at them with any care. The third room has some cutout models of London. The point of visiting the house is certainly made clear. Shakespeare, we are sonorously told, "shaped us, helped make us who we are," and we in turn are visiting the "house which helped turn him into the genius he became." This virtual experience, explains the designer, is to make the visit to the house more real. The tawdriness and meretriciousness are a good preparation for the gift shop with which you can be sure the tour will end.

The house itself is grimly fascinating. It is introduced by guides in costume ("No photographs, please"). The whole *stuck* of the presentation is the authenticity, not of the presence of Shakespeare himself, but of the typicality of what is on show for the period: "Authentically crafted, accurate replicas have been used to give a complete picture of a mid-sixteenth-century home like the Shakespeares'." This has some great innovations: the walls are covered with painted hessian, in surprisingly excitable, bright, and modern-looking designs, based on sixteenth-century patterns found in Oxford. Thanks to films and television we are used to thinking of Elizabethan interiors as whitewashed walls, with the occasional tapestry in royal palaces. These ornately patterned green and red or black and white burlap wall coverings startlingly change our perception of the living space, especially in the tiny rooms. Our eyes are flooded by color and shapes. The glove workshop has been duly reconstructed in the house ("You may touch the skins," says the guide), which is a good reminder of the closeness of living and working even for a middle-class Elizabethan family. There is the occasional piece of Elizabethan furniture by the walls, but much is "authentically crafted, accurate replicas." This too is nicely challenging. There is no reason why the wealthy Shakepeares wouldn't have been surrounded by new things, freshly cut wood, rather than antiques. The Elizabethans weren't, for themselves, the olden days.

But there are tacky, jarring moments galore. It would be churlish to regret the radiators and fire extinguishers: no one wants the experience of authenticity if it is freezing or dangerous. The bars on the windows are also to be expected, I suppose. But there is also a painful mistrust of the imagination. Each fireplace has a cheap plastic fire in it. The birth room has what looks like a plastic crib with a doll in it, no doubt to represent how a baby would have looked. The kitchen has two plastic pieces of chicken, eternally waiting cooking. "Oh for a muse of fire . . ."

The famous window, gray with scratchings by visitors of the past, has had to be taken out of its place in the birth room because it had become dangerously fragile. In 2000 it was moved to the room next door, where it is on display behind glass in a cabinet, a window behind a window. You can see Carlyle's name in bold cursive letters at the top of one of the panes, and a host of unknown names. The most recent we spotted was dated 1968, a shakily written inscription from the summer of love. I wonder when it became unacceptable to leave your mark on a heritage site? Especially one where others' signatures are so evident. The window is now beyond reach, a memorial of previous generations' habits, and I am sure that any attempt to start a new window would be swiftly punished. There's tradition and there's tradition. The control that the site insists on trying to exercise over your visit made me want to behave very badly indeed. My wife, my lawyer, is a good influence . . .

The most fascinating part of the whole house for me was the exhibition of pictures illustrating the history of the building itself. It had some nice images from before the nineteenth-century restoration, when the pub was a run-down establishment with few pretensions to cleanliness or heritage. But best of all are the pictures of the interior. In the nineteenth century, the upstairs room had bookcases with books in, some heavy antique furniture, pictures on every available wall space, and statues, mostly busts of Shakespeare in niches around the walls. It was a classic Victorian interior, cluttered, to our eyes, with books, as one would expect for the home of a famous author, a desk prominently

Shakespeare's House in 1850: before restoration when it was still a public house.

displayed (although there is no evidence Shakespeare wrote anything here, certainly not any of the plays or poems), and busts of Shakespeare, although all of these were obviously made well after his death. This was the Victorian Shakespeare, modeled by Victorian lights, at the height of the British Empire. This interior was completely redesigned in 1950, the year before the Festival of Britain, shortly after the end of the Second World War, when Britain was again reconsidering what it meant to be British in the world and to have an empire. The Victorian furnishings were all removed, although the desk remained, now pushed against the wall discretely. The walls of the room were whitewashed, the beams exposed. Now the building appeared austere, simple, restrained. There were very few pieces of old furniture. No books, no busts. It looked empty. Now, the twenty-first-century version—completed in 1999 for the millennium—has changed the interior again. Now there are the brightly colored walls, rich bed linens, reconstructions of toys and chairs in fresh, yellow wood. Once again the taste of reconstruction has changed. There is a strong sense of paradox here. We are here to feel the aura of Shakespeare, to get in touch with the presence of genius. This is authentic, we are told. But

Shakespeare's House in the 1950s: "I was not prepared to see it look so smug and so new. . . . It had been "restored," a word to strike terror into the heart of an antiquary, not to mention a man of taste," John Mounteney Jephson (1863).

the exhibition can't help but show us how the experience keeps being constructed and reconstructed for different generations of viewers, just as the house itself has been built and rebuilt over the centuries, as our tastes and ideas about the Elizabethans have shifted. As with the glass over the wattle and daub on the front of the house, we get no more than a glimpse, a cross-section, of the cultural construction of the image of Shakespeare's house. Herded through the house and back into the garden, where student actors were bellowing out snippets of the plays to applauding foot-weary visitors, it was even harder to imagine how the Victorian tourists could have become so excited by their pilgrimage here.

We strolled down Henley Street toward Holy Trinity Church, where Shakespeare is buried, down Church Street, where Marie Corelli's house stands—now the University of Birmingham's Shakespeare Institute. Church Street is one of the most beautiful streets in the town and, at least as we walked along, suddenly empty of tourists, except us (the signs to the church may direct you another way). One student darted out of the Institute and wandered off toward coffee. There is a whole row of Elizabethan alms houses, lurching, half-timbered, with a drunken overhang over the street. There are symmetrical Georgian houses in soft yellow stone. Some Victorian houses, solidly aging. The street curves gently, in all directions. There has been some preservation work, of course, and such beauty does not come without its costs, but unlike Henley Street, there is a sense of a living street, which has been allowed to develop over time without the distorting dictates of the tourist industry. It made the walk from the station feel all the more dispiriting.

The church is set amid tree-filled parks and an extensive old graveyard, and it has in the chancel twenty-six extraordinary fifteenth-century carved wood misericord seats, decorated with some mystical and some really rather secular figures. Shakespeare is buried in the floor before the altar—he was a church official as well as a rich landowner, hence the prime spot for him and his wife. In the wall above to the left is a memorial, put up during his wife's lifetime, a particularly rubicund and unflattering bust of the author, which high-minded Victorians excoriated as wholly unsuitable for the national poet. But, for once, no one pulled down the monument and replaced it with something more seemly. You can see what worried them: it is a bit too much like a garden gnome for comfort. The inscription on the grave is pretty hard to read from behind the barrier in front of it, but the words are printed above it:

> Good friend for Jesus sake forbeare
> To dig the dust encloased heare
> Bleste be ye man y^t spares thes stones,
> And curst be he y^t moves my bones

The curse has worked. Shakespeare has not been disinterred, nor even has such an excavation been suggested by the most gung ho literary archaeologist.

Although there are leaflets in twenty languages and an entrance charge to the chancel to see the grave, and although tour groups come through in their thousands, the church feels more low-key, quieter, and less tricked up than the birthplace; it is easier to see how one might, if so predisposed, be moved by the grave of the master. But even here the Victorian worshipers of the bard have stamped themselves over the physical site. The church Shakespeare saw did not look like this (the spire, for a start, postdates him). The extensive stained-glass windows are largely from the nineteenth century—with some particularly fine muted yellow and brown figures in the north aisle. If you look carefully, you can see a few pieces of medieval glass fragments reset in the windows immediately above them. The pulpit is Victorian marble, donated by Sir Theodore Martin in honor of his wife, the distinguished Shakespearean actress Helen Faucit, whose face is the model for Saint Helena, the central alabaster statue on it. (Saint Helena was the mother of Constantine, and she found the True Cross, among other relics, and should thus really be the patron saint of pilgrimages.) There are plenty of saints who would turn in their graves to think of a stage actress having such a glorified position in a church (but this is Stratford, where acting rules). The south aisle was once rather splendid, but it was taken apart when the organ was removed from there and a new grand instrument was placed high up above the nave in 1841, where it still is now. When this work was being undertaken, they dug up a huge altar stone. This had been buried during the Reformation to prevent its being destroyed by the Puritans. In the Victorian period, it was used to make a new stone, carved altar. This was a highly contentious act. The Oxford Movement was a radical group of Christians who wanted to bring the Church of England closer to a Catholic tradition and were deeply committed to ritual, especially rituals with altars and priestly garb—along with other church traditions, including chastity and even virginity. The Oxford Movement divided the church and led some of its members to become Roman Catholics: in the bitter nineteenth-century contests over faith and religious practice, an altar, especially a pre-Reformation altar, was a highly charged addition to a church. The windows, the altar, the redesign of the church in a more splendid, less Puritan form, all betoken a move toward a particularly High Anglican worship, a rejection, even, of standard Protestant liturgy. This move was normally undertaken in the name of the early church, a return to a historically authentic and thus time-honored practice. The love of Shakespeare and the love of the early church are both signs of a particular Victorian attitude to history in an age of progress.

Walking between the Victorian reconstruction of Shakespeare's house and the Victorian redesign of the interior of Holy Trinity Church is a journey through a particular Victorian engagement with the past. In the search for the history that mattered most for their national and religious identity, drastic rebuilding and redesign were par for the course. There was a boldness about Victorian planning that can take the breath away: imagine proposing today the removal of a medieval street to improve a view! It was done sometimes in the name of preservation, sometimes in the name of heritage, sometimes in the name of modern progress. Social policy rather than money dominated the rhetoric, if not the reality, of projects. This swirl of projects and ideas produced vitriolic disagreements: could a natural wonder like Thirlmere in the Lake District be changed to bring water to Manchester in the name of public health? Should an old building be allowed to fall away, naturally, as Ruskin demanded? Should it be rebuilt according to an original plan? Preserved as a ruin? Redesigned according to modern taste? It is not by chance that the great institutions of heritage—the National Trust, the Society for the Preservation of Ancient Buildings, the Ancient Monuments Protection Act—were all established in the Victorian era. Shakespeare's reinvention as the national poet comes hand in hand with the reinvention of the monuments of Shakespeare's life and death in Stratford. The Victorians needed their national poet, and they needed the shrines to embody their feelings for the past. Literature and the newly celebrated figure of the writer were absolutely integral to this fresh sense of the person in history.

Stratford proved the hardest place on our pilgrimage, for me at least, to feel any aura of genius, to sense the presence. There is too much bad acting, too much bad faith in the whole display, too much dressing up, even in a town dedicated to theater. Some five hundred thousand people visit the town each year, some two hundred thousand go to the church. I came away with no idea what the vast majority of those visitors made of their journey. In the house, most tourists had a slightly baffled air, as the guides told them potted tales of what would have been normal all those years ago. "Boys did wear girls' clothes for the first six years, so the dress on the bed is the sort of thing young William may have worn . . ." Most shuffled through in silence. Was this the awe and wonder that even the young Washington Irving summoned at the dust trod by Shakespeare's feet? I saw so little of the exhilaration, the sheer thrill that Victorian writers record as they stared at Shakespeare's fireplace, his final resting place. My first road trip to Stratford had been revelatory because the stage performances opened Shakespeare's plays to my imagination in a new way. Perhaps Shakespeare's birthplace still works like that for some. Perhaps a copy of a play, bought in the gift shop—because buying is what people do there—will turn out to change a life. But it felt more as though this was the heritage industry at full pelt, a packaged, organized, and thoroughly ersatz experience, a trip where the language of experience—"experience Shakespeare's world!"—is the least convincing promise of all. It made me question more sharply than ever before why visiting authors' houses meant so much to so many smart and sophisticated Victorians, and what we modern visitors could no longer share with them.

6

FREUD, ACTUALLY

MARESFIELD GARDENS is part of my language of everyday life. "We'll park on Maresfield," "Let's go up Maresfield." My sister went to school on Maresfield Gardens, at South Hampstead High School for Girls, and her daughters go there now. I gave a lecture on Greek tragedy there last year, which took me back with a certain melancholic longing to a schooldays production of *Antigone*, in which the unfeasibly attractive actresses came from my sister's school. Maresfield is still our cut-through from the station up to Hampstead village.

I was quite unaware then that Freud's house was on Maresfield Gardens, that Anna, his daughter, was still living there while I was loitering outside the school gates on the corner. I must have walked past the house hundreds of times. It wasn't made a museum until after I had left for university, and it is very strange indeed to imagine Anna Freud, a figure I had read so much about in later years, staring out at us from behind the net curtains while we were struggling through our adolescence.

"The place Freud inhabits"—that's a real question for modern society. We are on our way to the house he lived in for the last two years of his life, a 1920s red-brick Hampstead villa in a leafy street of suburban red-brick villas. But the place of Freud is another matter. It is easy enough to say that Freud is one of a handful of *Victorian* writers who define the modernity of the *twentieth* century (Marx and Darwin would be my other two). *The Interpretation of Dreams*, though it was actually published in 1899, has the date 1900 on its frontispiece, as though to inaugurate the new century. It is impossible for almost anyone in the modern West to talk about the self without paying some sort of homage to Freud. His ideas—the unconscious, for example—are part of how we all think about the basic psychic anatomy of the human being. The Freudian slip is a wholly familiar concept: I don't need to explain why my economist colleague was humiliated when he invited a rather attractive graduate to meet him in his orifice. Freud himself may have barely have used the term "phallic symbol," but everyone else does, and in a book or film it is rather hard to get a train into a tunnel without a certain knowingness. Freud is all around us, part of what everyone knows, absorbed, like air, into our world picture. As W. H. Auden put it, he is "a whole climate of opinion Under whom we conduct our different lives." Freud has proved again and again to be a writer who changes people's thinking, not least because he changes the whole notion of self-analysis—and, as Socrates said, the unexamined life isn't worth living.

But actually *reading* Freud has always been a somewhat rarefied activity. There is, of course, a high-level industry where every word of the master is picked over. At universities as well as in psychoanalytic training courses Freud is subject to the full panoply of professional study—criticism, schools of interpretation, conference papers, therapeutic training, and so forth. Freud, too, is a staple of literary and cultural criticism, which has led to a heated and ongoing debate between Freud and feminism, Freud and queer theory, Freud and art history: how—where—you see the phallus is a divisive issue. . . . But outside this high-level industry, it is a rather different story. "Freudian" is a term to bandy about, and only a social misfit (or an academic) would expect a bibliography as a follow-up. As with Marilyn Monroe, everyone is expected to know who Freud is. But Freud, actually, his elegant and gripping prose, doesn't get much read in the general run of things. Freud constantly hovers between being one of the most intensively studied texts of the century and one of the least read authors—but with the highest recognition factor. I can't think of anyone else who has quite this bizarre, iconic place in our culture (though Marx and Darwin come close second).

Now my wife most certainly has read Freud, and has a mother who is a Freudian analyst in New York. In New York, it is cool to have an analyst, even—just about—as a mother-in-law. You hear casually informative sentences like "I'll meet you at 1:00 after I see my analyst" or "my analyst lives on this block." You can ask friends how long they have been in therapy without provoking a fight. When my wife says of a friend, "Has she thought about getting some help?," this is not an inquiry about hiring a cleaner. In England, however, even in North London, psychoanalysis is still a subject for hushed tones. I have decided after much thought not to reveal here that I went through analysis as a child with an elderly German-accented woman in a red-brick villa in West Hampstead, though not, I hasten to add, on Maresfield Gardens—because I know in England I should feel quietly embarrassed not only by having had such a childhood experience but also by the social gaffe of mentioning it in public. The place of Freud in England is awkward—with the full, terrible weight of what "awkward" can mean amid the proprieties and fears of English social restraint. Bringing things into the open isn't really the English way: as a character in Somerset Maugham says, "sometimes I wish everything could be tacit." In Britain, to be a psychoanalyst or in analysis is always tinged with suspicion. So pilgrims to Maresfield Gardens, I suspect, won't be like the Brontë Society or the tour buses in Stratford.

Yet Freud's house fulfills the trajectory of this book perfectly, the icon at the end of a thematic journey. Shakespeare's birthplace was invented to give voice to a national identity, a truly English selfhood. The parsonage at Haworth in its moorland setting became a physical expression of the interiority of the self—a new sense of the passions and sensitivities swirling inside a woman in a restrictive and restricted social world. Wordsworth's cottages in the lakeside landscape are treated as a route to rediscover his journey into the self through memory, self-exploration, and friendship—the Romantic psyche. Scott's house was built as an embodiment of his baronial self-projection—as his novels and poems created a fictional world through which readers found themselves through the work of the imagination. All of our writers so far have been important for their Victorian readers precisely because they offered new articulations of the self, new journeys of self-discovery, new ways of finding oneself through words and the imagination. In each case, the house functions as a place where pilgrims could relive that experience and feel themselves in touch with the reality of the home out of which emerged the literature that so affected them. Freud, too, opened pathways into the life of the mind, through which the reader's self-awareness was fundamentally altered. And what image summons up the work of Freud more vividly and powerfully than the couch on which his patients lay in Maresfield Gardens?

When Freud was forced to leave Vienna by the Nazi regime—he was ransomed by his supporters in the West—he managed to bring out with him all of his art collection—no small achievement in view of the grasping confiscations usual for the period. This collection really mattered to him. It was primarily small ancient works from Greece, Rome, Egypt, and the East, which filled his consulting room, fringed his desk, and stood in glass-fronted cabinets around the walls. There are more than two thousand objects. Freud purchased around one every week of his collecting life, and spent hours buying, handling, describing, fondling the statuettes. It is strikingly bizarre that Freud never analyzed the passion of collecting, nor does he seem to have reflected on why it mattered so much to him to bring these things with him from Vienna, even when his life and the life of his family was under threat. Scott's things were significant to him because they came trailing clouds of glory from personal contact—not any old pen, but Napoleon's; not any old cup, but Bonnie Prince Charlie's. The other houses we have visited all reveled in this thrill of presence—the touch of the real. You are meant to be moved by Emily Brontë's teapot, the "silent witness" of her life. Shakespeare's chair was sold so many times because it had touched the buttocks of genius. Freud's collection is mostly quite different from this pattern. The pieces are generic, ancient things: a head from Egypt; a statue of Eros, the god of desire, from Greece; a sphinx. There are occasional named and specific objects, like the frieze of Gradiva from Pompeii, about which Freud wrote

Freud's House on Maresfield Gardens.

a beautiful essay—but the frieze is a cast, a copy. It is a memorial, but not tinged by the excitement of originality or authenticity. Freud brought all of these objects with him so that he could exactly recreate his Vienna consulting room in Maresfield Gardens.

When I grew up around Maresfield Gardens, there were plenty of elderly German-speaking men and women around, part of the soundscape of the city. There was a famous café on the corner by the main road where you could get coffee and strudel, and, if you were old and German, sit all day and talk about *die Heimat*, the home country. The smells and sounds of a lost home beguile refugees. But Freud's consulting room is something else. Freud is the great theorist of repetition, of the compulsions of routine. Yet when he left Vienna and came to London, he felt the need to make his office space exactly like the room he had left behind, with the same objects, the same lay-out, the same couch. He risked a great deal to bring out these objects to achieve this aim. Freud left Vienna in 1938, but recreated his Victorian study from

Europe here in modern Hampstead. At some level, Freud seems to be saying that there is a special link between his office space and how he works and lives.

At one level, it is easy to see how some of these objects would have a particular meaning for Freud. It isn't really a surprise to see a statue of the sphinx on the top of one of the cabinets, fundamental as she is to the myth of Oedipus, and fundamental as the Oedipus complex is for Freud's theories. The sphinx is the monster who threatened Oedipus, as she did all passersby, with a riddle. When he answered the question correctly—the answer was "man," that is, what Oedipus and all of us are—he saved the city from the monster, but he also took a crucial step toward having sex with his mother. Answering questions, as Freud knew better than anyone, is both compulsory and self-committing and hugely dangerous, even—especially—when you get the answer right. Analysts love questions. Nor is it hard to see why the god of desire, Eros, might sit on Freud's desk. Seeing desire everywhere was the threat and promise of Freud's theory in the minds of many of his earliest readers, often in a rather trivial manner—"a thing's a phallic symbol if it's longer than it's wide." But Freud's exposition of the self-deceptions, alibis, and misplaced certainties of the desiring subject is still the best antidote to the grim complicities and oversimplifications of the Hollywood rom-com in which we are constantly being encouraged to live.

But Freud actually used the little sculptures occasionally in treatment to make a point to the patient about how memories that were painful or obscene were buried in the mind, and how digging up the past was revelatory. This gives us a further insight into why these artworks mattered to Freud. Freud was obsessed with archaeology, one of the new and most exciting sciences of Victorian Europe. The discovery of the buried city of Pompeii in the eighteenth century had opened a new vista on the past of ancient Greece and Rome, and archaeology continued to make extraordinary discoveries throughout the nineteenth century, of which Schliemann's excavation of Homer's

Troy was the most glamorous. It is hard to overemphasize the importance of the classical past for the nineteenth century: classics took up 80 percent of the school curriculum in elite schools; it provided the ideals, political and artistic, for generations of young men and women, and, especially for the German-speaking world, the "tyranny of Greece over the German imagination" was pervasive—so pervasive that when Kaiser Wilhelm at the end of the century proposed major educational reforms, he felt the need to say, "We should raise young Germans, not young Greeks and Romans." Archaeology was so exciting because it suddenly revealed the glories of this idealized past as realities.

Archaeology as the science of the real, with its ability to prove what really happened in the past, was especially important when it came to the Bible. Textual scholars and radical theologians had offered damning, sophisticated, and scandalous challenges to the texts of the church tradition from the end of the eighteenth century onward. How could the stories of the Hebrew Bible be simply true? Was there any historical accuracy to the stories of the miracles of saints or even of Jesus? These questions threatened the whole establishment of the church, and through it the order of society itself: a religious war being enacted through scholarship. Biblical archaeologists set out to prove the Bible's veracity by excavating the material truth—and in many cases succeeded, at least to their own satisfaction. The store cities of Pithom and Ramses, described in the book of Exodus, were discovered, built with exactly the sort of bricks the Bible specified. (The excitement of this announcement faded as more research showed the bricks were actually typical of Egyptian building and the cities were probably wrongly identified . . .) The historical value of Homer's epics too had been roundly dismissed by trendy young academics. Schliemann's excavation of Troy itself seemed to strike a blow for the traditional truths of church and classics. The prime minister, Gladstone himself, also a Homeric and biblical scholar, introduced Schliemann at lectures for huge audiences: modern science had vindicated the truth of the past. Freud was typical of Victorian controversies when, late in life, in Maresfield Gardens, he hoped that his last and most wacky work, *Moses and Monotheism*, would be proved right by archaeological excavations in the East.

Freud was thrilled by archaeology, fascinated by its discoveries, and it helped form his thinking. He told Stefan Zweig that he had read more archaeology than psychology. Psychoanalysis, he wrote, clears away "psychical meaning layer by layer" which is like "the technique of excavating a buried city." He uses this analogy again and again. A psychoanalyst is like the explorer who excavates a lost ruin, to make "the stones speak." The psychologist "like the archaeologist at his excavation must uncover layer after layer of the patient's psyche before coming to the deepest, most valuable treasures." Reconstructing a scene from fragments of memories was like an archaeologist's piecing together a vase or fresco. "Just as the archaeologist builds up the walls of the building from the foundations that have remained standing," Freud writes, "and reconstructs the mural decorations and paintings from the remains found in the debris, so does the analyst proceed." He was particularly taken with the new scientific idea of stratification — the technique of understanding a site through different levels, "layer by layer." Freud saw himself as an archaeologist of the mind.

So, all around the couch, the office, the desk — archaeological objects. The poet and patient Hilda Doolittle (H.D.) wrote that Freud sat, "like a curator in a museum, surrounded by his precious collection." (It was to H.D. that Freud — and it could only have been Freud — said that his statue of Athena was "perfect only she has lost her spear" . . .) But Freud's collection tells a different sort of story from Scott's things. Scott cherished the scent of the individual, moments of a history with names, heroes, anecdotes. Freud's objects tell of a vast general history of mankind: the races of man, the history of religion. Like Darwin and Marx before him, Freud was a grand theorist of human nature, who saw evolution as a general pattern, a universal and universalizing account of how humans develop. Oedipus is every man and every man is Oedipus. Freud's collection encompasses the sweep of his vision. The contrast between Scott's things and Freud's artworks captures the transition of the nineteenth century. Scott's collection looks weird and backward to the end of the century, just as Freud's things would have been out of place in an early nineteenth-century study. What has changed is not just a style of display or a practice of collecting, but a view of history and a view of how a person is to be understood.

The house in Vienna had rather small, dark rooms in comparison with Maresfield Gardens; and there was, and still is, a splendid garden here in Hampstead, unlike in Vienna. In Vienna, the study and consulting room were separate; in Hampstead, the two rooms were one, with French windows opening onto the garden. But although there is more light and airiness in the study, its layout is a reconstruction of its form in Vienna. Freud built, as it were, the first museum of his earlier life. After his death, Anna did not work in her father's space, but established her own clinic in child development a few doors down at 12 Maresfield Gardens, where it still functions. Her relationship with her father, much chewed over in the history of psychoanalysis, was intense and competitive, supportive and corrective. Anna kept her father's study as it was for the next forty-three years of her single, working life, a museum of the founder of psychoanalysis and her dad. When she died, she intended the house to remain—become—a permanent museum, as it has: the house is no longer lived in but tidied into an exhibition of itself. The museum comes layered with a stratigraphic record of memorial: Freud of himself, Anna of her father, the museum trust of Anna's wishes. This is a museum three times over—which tells a story not just about museums but about the strange history of psychoanalysis. When we visit Haworth or, a more extreme case, Shakespeare's birthplace, the fantasy on show is that we are in touch with an authentic past, the presence of genius, which is why the story of reconstruction over subsequent years, and any doubts about authenticity, are kept rather quiet. But true to the archaeological principles of Freud, the Freud house proclaims its history over time, those acts of preservation and destruction that have passed down to us the icon of the couch, surrounded by his collection of antiquities. It may be a constructed museum three times over, in a suburban London street, but I find the link with a Victorian past all the more engaging for its actual, messy, but unbroken links back to Vienna in the nineteenth century, where a young Jewish doctor with a passion for ancient archaeology began to excavate the depths of the mind.

We strolled toward the house on Maresfield on the first truly sunny Sunday of summer. There is really no part of London more beautiful than Hampstead, especially in this sort of weather. So many of the houses on the hill are quirky mansions—"built for mistresses," I was always told, even as a child, and that louche luster has never left them for me—with red-brick turrets (to let down Rapunzel hair), and strangely shaped rooms looking onto gardens. The Heath seems to spread its greenness through the streets, and there is still a touch of bohemia around, although now only the very richest artists can afford to live here and the street cafes are crowded by very carefully and expensively dressed bohos. Freud's house is marked only by a couple of blue plaques on the wall and a very discreet poster board outside. The mums outside the school gates are regularly asked for directions by earnest seekers, hoping for more signs. One or two people are eying the entrance. A girl in jeans with a plastic badge hanging round her neck comes out to catch the sun and encourages us in. It is all very relaxed and open. But Freud was certainly right when he said, "We have it incomparably better than at Berggasse" in Vienna. This house is a large, beautiful villa and a seriously imposing piece of real estate. So what do North Londoners do? We immediately started to discuss the relative house prices, then and now, and wondered where Freud's money came from. As the trip's academic, I had to provide the answers. The house actually cost sixty-five hundred pounds in 1938 (and is worth several million today). His friend, Princess Marie Bonaparte, managed to smuggle out some of his assets in the form of gold bars through the Greek diplomatic bag, so he did not arrive penniless as so many refugees did, and he had family here to help. Unlike all the other houses on our pilgrimage, with Freud's place we were straight into the psychopathology of everyday life.

That sense of familiarity was uncannily present in the expansive hallway, which you come into before you reach the ticket counter in the conservatory. It smelled and looked like so many houses I had been in as I was growing up—the homes of my friends' grandparents in Hampstead Garden Suburb, slightly worn, consciously unmodern, slightly too pointedly for visitors, the whiff of wood polish and carpet and propriety. My own family lived in an architect-designed modern house of glass and wood, with a huge angular glass-roofed hall, with hanging balconies with black iron banisters and a three-story wall of modernist teak paneling. My friends' families had hallways that always felt like restricted, formal spaces, surrounded by closed wooden doors (the doors in our house were glass), and, as with Freud's hallway, they did not have the explosive modern art that my parents had bought. Freud has undistinguished, polite prints of the Villa d'Este and a view of Mount Fuji on the walls—memorials of trips taken and not taken—and, opposite you as you come in, a copy of a Rembrandt drawing of Moses holding the tablets of the ten commandments above his head.

Moses was a surprise. Freud had a deeply strained relation with his Judaism. He did not have his own sons circumcised, which is an extreme gesture even for the liberal, assimilated circles he moved in. He refused to have anything to do with organized or ritualized religion, and he forced his beloved wife, Martha, to give up the practices she was used to following from her own orthodox background. She lit Sabbath candles again after his death, a sad sign of his dominance in their relationship—or, as he would have seen it no doubt, of the persistence of religion in her mind and her return to premarriage securities. He was late for his own father's funeral because he had popped into the barber. There are no signs of Jewish life in Freud's house. He owned a menorah, the eight-branched candelabrum used at Chanukah, but only as an art object—it is a very rare thirteenth-century example and the most valuable object in his collection. We couldn't see it, or the two kiddush cups he owned, in the displays in the house. Yet Freud was acutely sensitive to any signs of anti-Semitism, which was virulent in Austria even before the advent of the Nazis. He was active, in Vienna, in B'nai B'rith, an organization of Jewish professionals. And he wrote obsessively about Judaism, his father's religion, particularly here at Maresfield Gardens, where he composed *Moses and Monotheism*. The Rembrandt print has Moses lifting the tablets aloft. Is he exultingly showing the commandments to the Israelites? Or is he about to smash them down in anger at their dancing around the Golden Calf? The houses I visited as a young guy all had some signs of their Jewishness, however much the owners struggled with the dynamics of assimilation: the candlesticks on the dresser, the menorah on the mantelpiece, the selection of books. Freud's hall has just this one pictorial sign of his intense ambivalence: a (Christian) image of the founding father of his religion perhaps about to smash the rules.

The audio guide at Freud's house is the most intense and full-scale production I have ever come across in a museum. You could write a pretty good student essay from it, and it takes a couple of hours—or two sessions of fifty minutes—to go through the house if you listen to all the tapes and look around with a modicum of care: there are seven separate talks for the study alone (books, objects, women, and so forth). The seriousness with which psychoanalysis takes itself and its history is uncompromisingly on show, and it couldn't be further from the Stratford Shakespeare Experience. The conservatory has a couple of hundred academic books on psychoanalysis on sale (as well as some grotesque Freud dolls and garish, fluffy "Freudian slippers," which would be a merciless present for a psychoanalyst mother-in-law). At the end, it feels rather exhausting: this is a museum with a message. The first guide is to the hallway. It creates a pleasing performative effect. We stood in the hall for a good while listening and shuffling and looking around, but not at each other, as if we were waiting for an appointment with the doctor, whose study and consulting room are off to the right.

The theatrical sense of buildup is fulfilled by the drama of entering Freud's lair. Carl Jung, Freud's onetime favorite pupil, described reading about Oedipus in the *Interpretation of Dreams* as being like "that peculiar feeling which arises in us if, amid the noise and tumult of a modern street, we should come across an ancient relic." In Jerusalem, I have had that feeling: in the midst of the traffic of modernity a sudden piece of broken wall around which some Bronze Age, biblical arrows had fallen, producing the vertigo of a glance down into the historical abyss. To turn into Freud's study is to take a vertiginous step back into a history: it is a strikingly memorable experience. The rooms are now hushed into cool shadedness, even in the summer sunlight, by the closed curtains and soft lighting. This darkness is for conservation, we are told, but the theatricality of the rooms was part of Freud's original design. The room is luxuriant and filled to overflowing. On the floors are lush oriental carpets; the walls are lined with old bookcases, also brought from Vienna, and everywhere the collection of what Freud called his old gods crowds the eyes. I had seen many pictures of the old Berggasse apartment, and many pictures of the collection, but the anatomized snaps do not prepare you for the overwhelming embrace of the space, the sense of entering into a world, Freud's world, where you have no role but the one the room creates for you.

The very richness of the scene makes you look here and there, trying to take in the objects as well as the overall atmosphere. But the eyes are drawn repeatedly to the center stage where Freud's couch and desk are placed, and specially lit up. The couch is covered with the most luxurious looking Persian rugs, textiles woven by the women of a nomadic Qashqai tribe of southern Iran, with deep, warm reds and ochers, intricately patterned and exquisitely textured. My wife, the psychoanalyst's daughter, captured the seduction of the stage set perfectly: "It's like a cocoon," she said wonderingly, wishing she could have had Sigi as her analyst, and then added, "a cross between an office and a bordello." It is certainly not like my mother-in-law's austere couch on the Upper East Side in New York, all bare lines and free from distractions—or any other analyst's office I have seen. At the end of Freud's couch there is table with a carved Roman head in a glass cabinet. At the end of my mother-in-law's, a telephone and pad. It is hard to imagine what it must have been like for Anna, Freud's daughter, after nearly twenty years of seeing her father go into the study with

The couch in Freud's consulting room: "Where the twentieth-century
person was born," Lisa Appignianesi.

strangers for hours every day, to lie down herself on the gilded couch
and begin her analysis. And then to start her own work on the traumas
of children in a bare bright room dominated by a glowering portrait
of her father.

Freud's desk is left with his glasses and book on it still, and the familiar spirits he greeted in the morning: the line of devotional statues.
The book on monotheism was penned here surrounded by the pagan,
polytheistic gods. An oddly discordant metal porcupine, a gift from
the one American trip Freud made, sits perkily by the writing pad,
a distinctly unmystic and disruptive beast. The chair, pushed back
from the desk, was designed personally for Freud by Felix Augenfeld.
Freud liked to sit with his legs over the arms of a chair to read, and
Augenfeld produced the high back and molded arms to accommodate
Freud's comfortably gangly pose. The chair is extraordinary, a sinuous
sculpture in itself, and it reminds me of nothing so much as a Cycladic
figurine, one of those early Greek statues that so influenced Picasso
and other modernist artists. To sit in it is to be hugged by a form that

Freud at his desk in Vienna: "Like a curator in a museum,
surrounded by his precious collection," H.D.

echoes the deep past of human representation—just as the statuettes
all around reach back into the history of human self-portrayal.

The books line the room, literature and archaeology as much as
psychology ("No Wordsworth," pointed out the still miffed wife tri-
umphantly), and the shelves are hung with photographs of the women
in Freud's life. Above the couch is a print of the famous painting
by Brouillet called *Un leçon clinique à la Salpetrière*, which depicts
Freud's great teacher Charcot demonstrating the effect of hypnosis on
a hysterical female patient. The short plump Charcot is looking calmly
at his all-male audience, who are staring with various expressions of

fascination and concern at the woman, collapsing backward into the arms of an assistant, her top loosely slipping. As a young and impressionable physician, Freud had nervously visited Charcot's house—he took cocaine to get him through the evening—and had written home afterward how wonderful the master's collection of antiquities had seemed to him, something for Freud to live up to. Charcot remained an influence on Freud, but it is still rather disconcerting to see this picture—with its eroticized focus on woman as an object in the hands of male doctors—above Freud's couch. It was not there in Vienna but elsewhere in the study; in Hampstead, it has replaced an image of the temples at Abu Simbel in Egypt. Who knows why the pictures changed places, but it makes a disconcerting juxtaposition to the opulent couch and sharpens our sense of the dodgy erotics of the "cross between an office and a bordello," and the dodgy gender politics at the heart of the history of psychoanalysis.

The room's lavish collection is overwhelming: it fills the visual space, offers too much to take in. The effect is doubled by the contrast with the rest of the house. The antiquities are only in the study. There, every space seems crowded with relics of antiquity; elsewhere Freud's house has his parents' clumpy painted cupboards, lightened by the occasional Biedermeier table, popular in the early nineteenth century in Vienna, the odd fruit bowl or flower vase. That is, the rest of the house has the feel of a bourgeois 1880s domestic environment, transported to Hampstead, already unfashionable by the time Freud was writing the *Interpretation of Dreams*, but still there fifty years later. After the study, everywhere else in the house feels empty, even thin. Anna's room upstairs has the loom at which she wove textiles to relax, along with her desk. But it is easy to see why one upstairs room is now dominated by a video playing loops of the Freud family's home movies, and another is dedicated to an exhibition space. These two rooms had nothing worth preserving in themselves, it seems, and are now just boxes in which other forms of memorialization take place. It looks like Freud's work is intently confined to the study, not allowed to invade the space of the house—a decision that for Freud, with his concern with boundaries, cannot be casual. Freud's office is like the unconscious of the house, a weird other place inside the bourgeois home.

So it is a touch of symbolic genius that has taken the frieze of Gradiva and moved it from the foot of the couch, where it had been on the wall in Vienna, and placed it on the broad door jamb between the study and the hall. Analyzing Jensen's story of Gradiva was Freud's first exercise in psychoanalytic literary criticism, a story that suitably enough focuses on a German archaeologist fixated on the image of a woman discovered in Pompeii, the high-stepping, flowing-robed Gradiva. The archaeologist's cure involves his discovering a real woman, his erstwhile neighbor, whose last name, Bertgang, means "someone who steps along brilliantly," as Gradiva means "the girl who steps along." Where better to put an image that sums up the curative transition from fantasy to reality, an image of "the girl who steps along," than by the door between the consulting room and the outside world, between the world of the statues and the world of the family?

The modern museum, however, has scattered the whole house with printed cards, with quotations from Freud's dream analyses, attached to objects already in the house, like a fireplace, or to objects carefully placed there, like a broken candle. So the celebrated dream of the burning child gets an outing by the fire, the dream of the broken candle by the broken candle on a plate nearby. I could see why they have done it: everyday objects are the stuff out of which dreams are made; there is a psychopathlogy of everyday things; our thoughts and intentions are revealed in the objects through which we make up our life. That is, of course, one reason why we love to snoop around other people's house, and why students are so tetchy about choosing the posters for their first-year accommodation. But I couldn't help feeling that the point was made rather too insistently and bluntly, in a way Freud would have found uncomfortably unnuanced: it dissipated the drama of Freud's construction.

On this sunny Sunday in Hampstead there were a steady trickle of visitors, maybe twenty at a time, in the house. The last month's visitors' book revealed that the vast majority of those who traveled here could call themselves pilgrims: they were psychology students, psychoanalysts, academics who came to see a place that loomed large in their imagination, to view a relic—the couch—touched by the full mystique of presence, the thrill of genius, the aura of history. We saw people walking slowly, staring intently, and discussing together. The occasional intense young man on his own, a mother and daughter. None of us had been before, and we were all fascinated and excited by it. Four Jews for Freud. . . . In Freud's study, for the first time on our pilgrimage, I was taken, like my Victorian pilgrims, by a feeling of amazement and moved by the absent presence of a powerful artist in and through the physical space he had inhabited. In part, this was because the space was precisely constructed as a stage set for the therapeutic process; in part because the scene is so overpowering in its multiplicity and richness; in part because the room, although reconstructed from Vienna, had a historical continuity and an integrity—it was always meant to be reconstructed and preserved like this. It is a powerfully evocative place, this place of Freud.

And yet, and yet, I found myself harboring two nagging doubts. First, I thought I knew that Freud would be rather pleased with my attention and my coming under his sway. When the poet H.D. came into the study and looked at his objects, he commented that she was the only patient to look first at the collection and second at him—but then they became friends, in a way that his own theories of transference should have debarred—and swapped antiquarian gifts and comments. Freud responded to people's response to his room, and he was jealous of his own fame. As I was affected by the room, I knew that that was exactly what I was meant to be feeling, and consequently a bit of me resisted. (Of course, said the analyst, the question is what are you actually resisting and at what cost?) But second, and less mean-spiritedly, I thought the analytical Freud would remind me that a collection is dead if it doesn't grow and change—as he sadly reflected as he put things on the shelf in England for the last time—and I should reflect why my response to this house didn't just show up my responses to all those other houses of dead relics. How different was my response here to the gooey imaginations I thought I disliked at heritage sites? Was I sure I knew the difference between the fakery of the Shakespeare experience and the tending of the Freud myth?

Well, why shouldn't a visit to the house of the founder of psycho-analysis leave you with a nagging question?

There is something of an anticlimax about the end of every pilgrimage. Like the new Beaujolais, one arrives. When the journeying is the thing, the conclusion is always tinged with loss. So perhaps I shouldn't have been the slightest bit perturbed to find myself finishing my journey, on a sunny Sunday in Hampstead, with my wife, on a street I had so often walked down as a child, outside a house that reminded me so vividly of my childhood, and discussing the man who had made childhood memories a key to understanding mental life, and whose work had been part of our separate and connected lives for so long. Standing inside in the semidarkness, a Jewish Greek scholar with an audio guide pressed to his ear, squinting at a model of the sphinx. . . . Where else would a pilgrimage like mine end up? We went back to our friends' place, and grilled steak on the barbecue, and sat in the sun.

I had learned a great deal on my pilgrimage, about writers, their houses, and the development of heritage, celebrity, and literary cul-ture, over the nineteenth century and today. But what surprised me most about the whole journey—which included the research and the writing—turned out to be how distracted I became by the odd plea-sures and fears of self-exposure, for all that I knew before that pilgrim-age encourages such revelations, especially a pilgrimage to destinations like these. We are none of us very good at thinking about how writers' lives affect our response to their work. Does it—should it—matter to us, when we listen to Wagner that he was a foul anti-Semite? Does it change our pleasure in his music? Does the fact that Heidegger was an active member of the Nazi party alter how we read his philosophy of time? Should Freud's treatment of his wife and daughter inform how we read his theories of gender? I don't think there are any straightforward answers to those questions—or at least any *satisfactory* straight-forward answers. As a scholar, in the name of objectivity, principled methodology, accuracy, I have been trained to be highly suspicious of the personal voice in my work—both when it is exhibited and when it is wholly repressed. (My dear friend Teresa Brennan, the psycho-analytic feminist critic, who was killed in a hit-and-run accident a few months after she had adopted a young child, coined the fabulous term "sado-dispassionate" to capture that particular male academic commitment to cold, abstract argument as a way of dealing with the passions and personal politics of her field. It is a term that should catch on.) I had begun my pilgrimage not understanding why anyone would care about a writer's house. Surely the book's the thing. I had gradually been sucked into worrying about how a writer's life—for which the house is the physical embodiment—becomes part of how we understand the writing. And, with a modicum of self-awareness, which is the besotting lure of every pilgrimage, this inevitably means angsting about how my own life is part of this my writing, then. The angst is a bit like the pleasures and fears of a date: once you start thinking too much about how everything you say reveals more than you want and less than you mean to say about yourself, it can lead to stammering, blushing, and head-slapping foolishness. It isn't obvious how one should put one's self into words.

"Middle child, pushy Jew, overintellectual, North London . . . ," began my wife, who knows. That and more, no doubt. But Walter Scott seems to get it about right. Even as you proclaim yourself "Safe behind walls," there is always a revelatory anagram of your self in the mottos you hide behind.

HOW TO GET THERE

It is extremely easy to visit all these houses. I tried to stick to trains and bicycle, but I will give here directions by both public transport and by car. Each has a small admissions charge, and each has a good website with up-to-date information about other events, such as poetry readings, festivals, conferences, taking place. It is possible to visit all in sequence or to make several trips. You could do the whole journey in six rather rushed days, but as Scott said "You must not think our neighborhood is to be read in a morning, like a newspaper. It takes several days of study for an observant traveler that has a relish for auld world trumpery."

Abbotsford

Abbotsford is open March 15–October 31 from 9:30 a.m. to 5:00 p.m., though it opens at 11:00 a.m. on Sundays in March, April, May, and October. Plans are afoot for a new visitor center, but as we go to press, it is not yet built.

Abbotsford House is two miles from Melrose on the B6360. The easiest route from Edinburgh is the A7 toward Galashiels and Selkirk. From Galshiels either continue toward Selkirk on the A7 for two and a half miles and then turn left on the B6360. Abbotsford is on the left, with the carpark on the right. Or take the A6091 at Galashiels toward Melrose and, after seven hundred meters, at the roundabout on the A6091 urn right onto the B6360. Abbotsford is a quarter mile down the road here on the right, with parking on the left.

For public transport take the X95 bus from Waterloo Place in Edinburgh to Galshiels. It takes an hour and twenty minutes. From

Galashiels, you can take a bus to Tweedbank, which is the roundabout on the A6091, then walk the quarter mile up the B6360. The walk from Galashiels to Tweedbank is not particularly attractive and takes around forty minutes.

Dove Cottage and Rydal Mount

Dove Cottage is open daily from 9:30 a.m. to 5:00 p.m. (4:00 p.m. in the winter, until the beginning of March). It is closed January 4–29.

Rydal Mount is open March 1–October 31 from 9:30 a.m. to 5:00 p.m. It is open Wednesday through Sunday 11:00 a.m. to 4:00 p.m. during November, December, and February and closed during January. But beware: if there is a tea party booked, the house will be shut to visitors (although the grounds open). It is hard to know when these parties are; so it is best either to check by phoning ahead or to visit in the morning.

Both Dove Cottage and Rydal Mount are just off the A591, which is the main Kendall to Keswick road. If you are driving from the south, the easiest rote is to leave the M6 motorway at junction 36 and follow the signs for Kendall, Windermere and Ambleside—this is the A591. Both sites are signed from the road between Ambleside and Grasmere. If you are coming from the north, leave the M6 at junction 40, follow the signs to Keswick (A66) and then to Grasmere and Ambleside (A591).

Or take the train to Windermere. Then cycle or walk the six miles to Rydal or nine to Dove Cottage along the A591. There is a good bicycle rental shop right outside Windermere Station.

Haworth Parsonage

The parsonage is open 10:00 a.m. to 5:30 p.m. from April to September, and 11:00 a.m. to 5:00 p.m. from October to March. It is closed December 24–27 and January 4–31.

The parsonage is on Church Street at the top of the village: it is well signed in the village itself, and there are several car parks. From London, take the A1 or the M1 toward Leeds, and take the M62 to the M606 junction. At the roundabout there take the A58 toward Halifax. At Halifax take the A629 (Ovenden Road). Turn left onto the A6033/B6142, the Haworth Road, which turns into the B6142, Lees Lane, which you follow down and round through the village up to the parsonage.

The train to Keighley (change at Leeds) will leave you with a walk or cycle of four miles. Leave Keighley on the Oakworth Road (B1643) [take Cavendish Street opposite the station, turn left and right after the cinema], go past the Branshaw golf club. The road turns into Keighley Road after a mile or so. At Oakworth turn right on Providence Lane which becomes Mytholmes Lane which leads up to the parsonage.

Stratford and Shakespeare's Birthplace

The birthplace house is open all year except Christmas Day: 10:00 a.m. to 4:00 p.m. from November to March; 9:00 a.m. to 5:00 p.m. from April to June, and in September and October; and 9:00 a.m. to 6:00 p.m. in July and August.

To drive, take the M40, and exit at exit 15 (Warwick), onto the A46 south east signed to Stratford (the Warwick Road). Either branch off at the A439 (Warwick Road) which takes you straight into Stratford; or continue on the A46, a better road, till you turn left on the A3400 (signed to Stratford). Both bring you into town: there are well signed car-parks and and signs for the birthplace and other sites.

From the station, walk up past Mary Arden's farm onto Alcester Road, cross over the crossroads on to Greenhill Street, left up Windsor Street and right onto Henley Street: maybe six hundred yards altogether.

Freud's House

The house is open Wednesday to Sunday noon to 5:00 p.m.

You could drive, but is not easy to park nearby, though you may be lucky on a Sunday.

It is best to take the tube, either to Finchley Road. (Turn right as you come out of the station along the Finchley Road, cross over at the lights, and climb up the stairs at Trinity Walk (fifty yards from the station) which leads you onto the corner of Maresfield Gardens: turn left and go to number 20. You can also walk down the hill from Hampstead tube—down Fitzjohns Avenue, right on to Nutley Terrace, left onto Maresfield Gardens, but this is fifteen minutes walk rather than five.

FURTHER READING

There are no footnotes in this series, and I have not therefore been able to acknowledge on the spot the many occasions when I have drawn on my colleagues' expertise and the work of other scholars. This section of further reading does not include books by the authors whose houses I visited, which are easily available, but does include the sources I found most useful in writing this book. There are many other I could have listed, of course, including lots of literary criticism and more general books on Victorian history. What I have listed here is a mix of Victorian discussions and modern analyses. I have marked with asterisks ten modern books of broad interest that I think are especially good reads.

Ackroyd, P. *Shakespeare: The Biography*. London, 2005.

Armstrong, R. *A Compulsion for Antiquity: Freud and the Ancient World*. Ithaca, NY, 2005.

Barker, S. ed. *Excavations and Their Objects: Freud's Collection of Antiquity*. Albany, 2006.

Bourke, R. *Romantic Discourse and Political Modernity: Wordsworth, the Intellectual and Cultural Critique*. New York, 2003.

Bowler, P. *The Invention of Progress: The Victorians and Their Past*. Oxford, 1989.

Brooke, S. *Dove Cottage: Wordsworth's Home from 1800–1808*. London, 1890.

Brown, B., ed. *Things*. Chicago, 2004.

*Brown, I., and G. Fearon. *Amazing Monument: A Short History of the Shakespeare Industry*. London, 1939.

Burke, J. *The Gods of Freud: Sigmund Freud's Art Collection*. Sydney, 2006.

*Buzard, J. *The Beaten Track: European Tourism, Literature and the Ways to 'Culture' 1800–1918*. Oxford, 1993.

Cheetham, J. K. *On the Trail of William Shakespeare*. Edinburgh, 2006.

Cliff, N. *The Shakespeare Riots: Revenge Drama and Death in Nineteenth-Century America*. New York, 2007.

Crockett, W. S. *Abbotsford*. London, 1905.

———. *The Scott Country*. London, 1905.

Deelman, C. *The Great Shakespeare Jubilee*. London, 1964.

Elnser, J., and R. Cardinal, eds. *The Cultures of Collecting*. London, 1994.

Fraser, R. *Charlotte Bronte*. London, 1985.

Fritzsche, P. *Stranded in the Present: Modern Times and the Melancholy of History*. Cambridge, MA, 2004.

Fuss, D. *The Sense of an Interior: Four Writers and the Rooms That Shaped Them*. New York, 2000.

Gagnier, R. *Subjectivities: A History of Self-Representation in Britain, 1832–1920*. Oxford, 1991.

Gamwell, L., and R. Wells, eds. *Sigmund Freud and Art: His Personal Collection of Antiquities*. London, 1989.

Gaskell, E. *The Life of Charlotte Bronte*. London, 1857.

*Gay, P. *The Naked Heart: The Bourgeois Experience from Victoria to Freud*. London, 1995.

*Gere, C. *Knossos and the Prophets of Modernism*. Chicago, 2009.

Gérin, W. *Anne Brontë*. London, 1959.

———. *Branwell Brontë*. London, 1961.

———. *Charlotte Brontë: The Evolution of Genius*. Oxford, 1967.

Gill, S. *Wordsworth and the Victorians*. Oxford, 1998.

Gilman, S. *Freud, Race and Gender*. Princeton, 1993.

*Girouard, M. *The Return to Camelot: Chivalry and the English Gentleman*. New Haven, 1981.

Gordon, L. *Charlotte Brontë: A Passionate Life*. London, 2008.

Halliday, F. *The Cult of Shakespeare*. London, 1957.

Halliwell-Phillipps, J. *Outlines of the Life of Shakespeare*. 5th ed. London, 1885.

Hazlitt, W. *Table-Talk: Essays on Men and Manners*. London, 1821–1822.

Hendrix, H., ed. *Writers' Houses and the Making of Memory*. London, 2008.

Hunter, R. E. *Shakespeare and Stratford-upon-Avon*. London, 1864.

Irving, W. *Abbotsford and Newstead Abbey*. London, 1835.

———. *The Sketch Book of Geoffrey Crayon, Gent*. Ed R. Rust. Boston, 1978.

Jarvis, R. *Romantic Writing and Pedestrian Travel*. London, 1997.

Jones, G. *The First Jubilee Oration upon the Life, Character and Genius of Shakespeare*. London, 1836.

Koselleck, R. *Futures Past: On the Semantics of Historical Time*. Trans. K. Tribe. Cambridge, MA, 1985.

Langan, C. *Romantic Vagrancy: Wordsworth and the Simulation of Freedom.* Cambridge, 1995.

Lee, S. *A Life of William Shakespeare.* 3rd ed. London, 1898/1922.

Levine, P. *Amateur and Professional: Antiquarians, Historians and Archaeologists in Victorian England, 1838–1886.* Cambridge, 1986.

Mackenzie, R. S. *Sir Walter Scott: The Story of His Life.* Boston, 1871.

*Mandler, P. *The Fall and Rise of the Stately Home.* New Haven, 1997.

Maxwell-Scott, Hon. Mrs. M. M. *Abbotsford: The Personal Relics and Antiquarian Treasures of Sir Walter Scott.* London, 1893.

Miller, L. *The Bronte Myth.* London, 2001.

Mitchell, R. *Picturing the Past: English History in Text and Image, 1830–1870.* Oxford, 2000.

Mole, T. *Byron's Romantic Celebrity: Industrial Culture and the Hermeneutic of Intimacy.* Basingstoke, 2007.

———, ed. *Romanticism and Celebrity Culture, 1750–1850.* Cambridge, 2010.

Moncrief, W. *Excursion to Stratford-upon-Avon.* London, 1824.

Moody, R. *The Astor Place Riot.* Bloomington, 1958.

*Ousby, I. *The Englishman's England: Taste, Travel and the Use of Tourism.* Cambridge, 1990.

Poole, A. *Shakespeare and the Victorians.* London, 1994.

Pope-Hennesy, U. *The Laird of Abbotsford: An Informal Presentation of Sir Walter Scott.* London, 1932.

Rogers, E., E. Eustis, and J. Bidwell. *Romantic Gardens: Nature, Art and Landscape Design.* New York, 2010.

Rudnytsky, P. *Freud and Oedipus.* New York, 1987.

Salvesen, C. *The Landscape of Memory: A Study of Wordsworth's Poetry.* London, 1965.

*Schivelbusch, W. *The Railway Journey: Trains and Travel in the 19th Century.* Trans. A. Hollo. Oxford, 1981.

*Solnit, R. *Wanderlust: A History of Walking.* New York, 2000.

Vance, N. *The Sinews of the Spirit: The Ideal of Christian Manliness in Victorian Literature and Religious Thought.* Cambridge, 1985.

*Watson, N. *The Literary Tourist.* Basingstoke, 2006.

Wheler, R. B. *History and Antiquities of Stratford-upon-Avon.* London, 1806.

PHOTO CREDITS